Volume 5 LONDON

ADAM GOLDBERG
Editor in Chief

DANIELA VELASCO
Creative Director

ELYSSA GOLDBERG
Executive Editor

BONJWING LEE
Copy Editor

-

CONTRIBUTORS
Aaron Bernstein
Aiste Stancikaite
Ferhat Dirik
Georgie Carroll
Imogen Lepere
Isabel Lea
Jacqueline Larkin
James Hansen
John Moore
John Surico
Jonathan Shipley
Lucia Ammadeo
Maggie Spicer
Maureen M Evans
Megan Krigbaum
Monique Aimee
Neha Pearce
Sabrina Sucato
Sarah Kollmorgen
Shanthy Sooriasegaram
Sharon Farrow
Stuart Milne

WELCOME

London was never known for its food—that is, until recently. A city where culinary highlights were once bangers and mash, fish and chips, and shepherd's pie has gone from intentional international culinary avoidance to a culinary destination. London, without a doubt, has become one of the great eating capitals of the world.

What makes eating in London so interesting is not a single unifying movement. Rather, it is a loose patchwork of new ideas and techniques, many imported from elsewhere, each focused on maximizing flavor.

The spectrum of dining options is wide-reaching, from fine dining to late-night doner kebab. West of London is the home of one of the pioneers of molecular gastronomy, Heston Blumenthal's The Fat Duck. With three Michelin stars, it serves food that evokes the senses, like the famous "Sounds of the Sea," in which fresh shellfish are presented alongside an iPod and headphones inside a conch shell to transport you to the sea. In Shoreditch is Imad's Syrian Kitchen, where a Syrian refugee serves supper club dinners in his upstairs apartment kitchen. Somewhere in between is the new guard of natural wine bars and a devotion to "nose-to-tail" eating where, at restaurants like St. John, Fergus Henderson lets nothing go to waste. It is this variety and the diversity of its cooks that make London's dining scene unique.

In keeping with this theme, writing in our London issue bounces between British- and American-English, so we can hear our contributors voices as they are. From hunting for British truffles to clinking pint glasses in pubs and returning home for Sunday roasts, *Ambrosia*, Volume 6: London takes a look at London's food scene past, present, and future.

Adam Goldberg
Editor in Chief

The Hunt for Britain's Black Diamonds

Words by Shanthy Sooriasegaram
Photography by Stuart Milne

"Presently, we were aware of an odour gradually coming towards us, something musky, fiery, savoury, mysterious,—a hot drowsy smell, that lulls the senses, and yet enflames them,—the truffles were coming!"
– William Makepeace Thackeray

The truffles are indeed coming…and these elusive delicacies are no longer exclusive to French dining tables, nor the famous truffle producing hills of Northern Italy. Unbeknown to many, they can be found right here in Britain, growing natively and in abundance.

Truffle connoisseurs have long praised the French Perigord black and the Italian white truffle—both of which experience a demand so high that it cannot be met, resulting in prices that can rise in excess of €10,000 per kilogram. Though lesser known than its continental cousins, for those in the know, the British 'Summer Truffle' *Tuber Aestivum* and the British 'Autumn Truffle' *Tuber Uncinatum*, are also prized for their culinary value.

The subtly sweet, earthy and nutty flavor of summer truffles, which ripen in early May and continue to fruit until autumn, is said to be less pronounced than the Italian and French varieties; but, for those who find truffle overpowering, this can be a bonus. British autumn truffle, on the other hand, has a deeper, more intense flavor, commanding a higher price than the summer pickings. DNA sequencing has revealed that the two British varieties are in fact the same species, but the time at which they are harvested lends them a different taste and intensity. Both varieties are best served as a garnish, shaved onto dishes like risotto or pasta. Alternatively, they can be used as a powerful means of infusing and enhancing even the simplest ingredients, such as eggs and cheese. The key is to be more generous with it than you would with the most prized continental varieties. It might take a whole British truffle to equal the impact (albeit, sadly, not the flavour) produced by a few shavings of the Perigord black or Italian white truffle, but when built up generously in this way, British truffle is perfectly capable of achieving the exquisite sensory experience that has kept truffles in high demand since Roman times.

For centuries, truffles have mystified those who stumble upon them. Early attempts to explain these peculiar underground growths concluded that they were a product of miraculous origin—for what other way could these oddities bearing no stem, leaves, or roots have been formed? The Roman poet Juvenal attributed the birth of the truffle to a thunderbolt thrown by Jupiter at the roots of an oak tree. As a mythical character known for his conspicuous sexual activity, the link to Jupiter established the truffle's long-surviving reputation as an aphrodisiac—a reputation reinforced by its deep, musky aroma and of course by the euphoria described by those who have feasted upon them. In fact, the only thing sensually at odds with this association is the undeniable ugliness of the truffle. To look upon it aesthetically is to see a hard, potato-shaped object, with a lumpy, wart-covered exterior. Emerging from the soil (as they sometimes do), to the uninitiated, they could easily be dismissed as dried animal feces.

That truffles are so coveted is partly due to how elusive they are—not only for their rarity (their natural habitat abroad is in decline due to human impact on the environment), but also because they are so challenging to find. As Marion Dean notes in *Discovering the Great British Truffle*, "As the truffle forms, it is hidden from view. When the truffle matures, it is hidden from view. Dwell on these thoughts for just a moment or two. I am sure you will begin to appreciate some of the problems connected with truffles."

Herein lies the role of the domestic animal in the truffle hunt. The primary indicator as to where a truffle is hidden (particularly a ripe truffle that is ready to harvest) is its aroma—one which, when buried underground, requires a nose more sensitive than a human's.

It's said that truffles contain androstenol, a sex hormone that is found in the saliva and sweat of male pigs, making truffles particularly appealing to sows. For this reason, historically, female pigs were often employed for the hunt. However, many truffle hunters lost not just the majority of their bounty to these greedy

and difficult to control animals, but also their fingers too. Dogs on the other hand proved more willing to hand over their finds in exchange for an appropriate reward. Although training them requires great tenacity on the part of the dog and handler, dogs are far more responsive than pigs and generally make better companions on long days out in the woods.

In Britain, the first documented truffles were found in Northamptonshire over three centuries ago. By the 19th century, British truffling was a small but thriving cottage industry. The south-facing, broad-leafed woodlands of Southern England, with their high-pH soils and free-draining, chalk bedrocks, provided an idyllic environment for truffles. The warmth of the summer sunshine together with the moisture brought by summer showers ensured the truffles reached maturity. Amongst the root systems of the coppiced beech, oak, hazel, hornbeam, lime, and birch trees that they favour, the truffles enjoyed a symbiotic relationship with their host trees, drawing energy through carbohydrates from their roots in exchange for water and nutrients.

Historically, the town of Winterslow was the epicentre of the British truffle trade. It was home to Britain's most famous truffle hunter Eli Collins, who once uncovered a whopping two-pound truffle. So large and spectacular was this find that it was gifted to Queen Victoria. His son Alfred is said to have been Britain's last great professional truffle hunter, retiring in the 1930s. At the peak of the trade, Winterslow's post office became known for the scent of truffles it bore, seeping from the steady flow of tubers passing through it as the Collins' bounty was boxed up and sent off around the country.

A number of factors are said to have contributed to the industry's decline—most notably the Second World War, which claimed the lives of many of the last truffle hunters. Growing conditions for fungi also deteriorated as ancient woodlands were felled to make room for roads. In the case of the Collins family, however, it was Alfred's unexplained decision not to pass on his knowledge that brought an end to his family legacy, much to the regret of his Wiltshire-based ancestors today. Collins took to his grave not just the knowledge of how to locate and unearth truffle, but also a precious mental map of British woodlands and the secret, undocumented locations in which truffles could be found.

Melissa Waddingham, a professional truffle and mushroom hunter based in Sussex, near London, is part of a new generation of foragers committed to reviving this knowledge and rediscovering the lost map of British truffles.

It was a combination of her love for the outdoors and a desire to put wholesome, organic food on the family dining table that led Waddingham to start foraging. Hearing whispers of truffle finds along the South Downs circa 2004, she was presented with the ultimate in mushroom hunting challenges: Could she really discover a truffle for herself right here in Britain? Stories of truffle discoveries were rare, and the majority of truffling tales were ones of years of fruitless hunting, even with the help of trained hounds. Convinced she would never find the elusive treasure with just her human senses to guide her, she made a promise to herself that if she ever did, she would immediately buy and train her own truffle hound.

"In my ignorance, on my first hunt I got out a map and circled the area I thought I'd find truffle for all the various different reasons I was armed with. I thought that wood looks big enough, it's facing the right way, it's chalk soil, it's got the right tree species…it ticked all the boxes. I can't reveal the precise location but when I got there, I thought eurgh…it was heavily dog walked, not quite what I'd expected."

"I was walking and came to this beautiful, majestic avenue of beech trees. I got on my hands and knees and started looking around this almighty tree. I was going through the leaves. I promise you after about ten minutes this thing sort of bounces out of the leaf litter and rolls away from me."

"It looked like the truffles in the books—

but there was no smell." Twenty minutes of continued searching revealed another dozen or so similar growths. The absence not just of the pungent odour one associates with truffles, but of any smell at all left her confused as to what exactly it was she had found. Together with some friends, she drove to a nearby pub for an uncertain, half-celebration, leaving the unidentified bounty in the car. Half a pint later, they returned.

"When we opened the car door, the smell was just bonkers. We just knew it was truffle." Elated, the group ran back to the pub for a second, far more enthusiastic celebration. With hindsight and experience to guide her, Waddingham notes that the smell of a truffle is constantly changing, developing as they ripen—so in fact, when discovering truffles early in the season, the aromas may be subdued. "What I should have done was sniff the soil", she says—for there she would have found a distinct and unmissable sweetness, indicative of truffles.

True to her promise, Waddingham now has three working dogs, Zebedee, Ela and the newest addition, Aesti (named after the British summer truffle *Tuber Aestivum*). All three were trained by Waddingham to hunt for truffles—a service she now offers to other dog owners alongside her education programmes and group forages.

Despite being licensed as a professional forager, Waddingham prefers to harvest only for personal consumption. Even when on a group foray, she sticks within the kilo-and-a-half legal limit set for one individual, splitting this allowance between the group.

Overharvesting a site poses risks to future supplies. For this reason, and to prevent unlicensed foraging that might damage the delicate ecosystems in which truffles thrive, professional foragers continue to keep secret the locations in which truffles have successfully been harvested, meaning that even today, the truffle industry remains one in which secrecy abounds.

Waddingham not only always leaves some truffles behind in the ground, but she also makes a point of gathering and drying all her excess truffle scrapings as one might do with vegetable peel. She returns these precious spores to the woodlands where they wait like seeds—a process which mimics the natural ecosystem in which animals would eat the truffles and redistribute the spores through their droppings.

British truffles prefer shallow soils, lending themselves to the odd spontaneous find as they occasionally rise to the surface. Consequently, they have been found in some of the most unlikely corners of Britain.

When questioned on their presence in London, Waddingham replies assertively; "Oh yes, there is truffle in London." For obvious reasons, Waddingham will not reveal the specifics of these locations, though she does note that one is a protected area—a Site of Scientific Interest (SSI)—on which truffle should not be hunted. Other finds have been documented in places as bizarre as school playgrounds and even in Wormwood Scrubs (a West London prison).

On an academic level, the holy grail of truffle research has been focused on their artificial cultivation. Spore-infected trees are now readily available, and where conditions are right, these trees have borne plentiful British truffles among their roots. In 2017, in an unexpected development during an experiment to monitor the growth of inoculated Mediterranean oak trees in Wales, a Perigord black truffle (one of the most highly valued species in the world) was successfully harvested—the first time such a high value species has successfully been grown in Britain. Such developments indicate Britain's climate is warming and becoming more favourable to truffle.

With provenance becoming a more and more important consideration for restaurants, top London chefs are increasingly sourcing British truffles for their menus. The Harrow, a Michelin-starred restaurant in Little Bedwyn, was one of the first restaurants to feature British truffle on its menu back in 2004 after a local landowner unexpectedly unearthed around £33,000 worth of summer truffle and took it to head chef Roger Jones for identification.

The successful cultivation of truffles from spore-infected trees has enabled restaurants to have a continual supply from flourishing British plantations. But alongside this steady stream, truffle suppliers such as James Painter of Sybaritic Ltd are also ensuring the old tradition of the individual hunter and their hounds survive. Four years ago, he bought his first wild British truffle direct from Waddingham—meeting her at a motorway service station where he negotiated a deal for the freshly unearthed truffle sitting in her car boot. Since then he's done many more deals in car parks and service stations across the country—directly with the truffle hunters themselves. In season, he now collects 10 to 15 kilos of British truffle a week in this way.

As ripe truffle is best consumed fresh, the ability to get British truffle from ground to plate within a matter of hours (unlike the truffle imported from Europe) is a game-changer, completely transforming the way in which truffles can be experienced in London restaurants. For those wishing to try it, Chef Mark Hix, celebrated for his unrivalled use of ingredients with provenance, is a regular client of Painter's, and fresh, wild, British truffle picked by the likes of Waddingham often makes it onto the menu of his London restaurant Hix Soho.

But before you rush to order a portion of truffle fries, or swoon over the aroma of truffle rising from the oil on your prosciutto-covered pizza, a word of warning on the use of truffle *oils*: real truffle oil is as rare and expensive as real truffles. In fact, most truffle oil—up to 98%, according to some experts—is entirely synthetic, containing no truffle whatsoever. What it does contain is laboratory-produced 2,4-dithiapentane—just one of the hundreds of aromatic molecules found in real truffles. Sadly, the one-dimensional flavor of synthetic truffle oil, described by Chef Gordon Ramsay as "one of the most pungent, ridiculous ingredients ever known to chefs" has become widely (and falsely) accepted as representative of the true truffle experience.

The problem with truffle oil is that there is no easy way to commercially produce the genuine article, as truffle will spoil if left in oil, carrying a risk of Botulism—which, although rare, can be fatal. The only way to safely get around this is to boil the truffle to such a high degree that any flavor would be lost, making the endeavour a pointless one—hence synthetic oils filling this gap in the commercial market.

But, if you are lucky enough to actually find and harvest your own British truffle as you wander through the woodlands, you can of course infuse your own oil. Just be certain to consume it quickly whilst the truffle is still fresh. Or better still, forget the oil and make yourself a batch of truffle butter which can be frozen easily and therefore safely stored—melt this into mash or generously rub it under the skin of a free-range chicken, allowing the fats to act as a glue for the magnificent odour—and indeed, you will witness how truffle can make the very simplest of things divine.

–

Melissa Waddingham.

The Proof is in the Puddings

Words by Jonathan Shipley
Illustrations by Sharon Farrow

Praise be the mighty pud. "They bake them in the oven, they boil them with meat, they make them 50 different ways," noted French writer François Maximilien Misson in the 1690s. "Blessed be he who invented pudding for it is manna that hits the plates of all sorts of people." He continues, a sermon for the meats and sweets. "A manna, better than that of the wilderness because the people are never weary of it. Ah, what an excellent thing is an English pudding!"

Praise be, indeed. There is the Eton mess and the sponge; the crumble and the Christmas pudding; the Queen of Puddings and the spotted dick; the trifle and the jam roly-poly. There are as many puddings as there are Londoners eager to eat one. But trying to pin down the true definition of a pudding is as difficult as pinning a pudding to a wall.

According to the English Oxford Living Dictionary, a pudding is either "a cooked sweet dish served after the main course of a meal" or "a sweet or savory steamed dish made with suet and flour." Hence the difficulties in defining it. Perhaps David Dias, the pastry chef at London's Basement Sate, has the most apt definition: "Pudding is the food for your soul. You don't eat pudding because your body needs it, but because your body wants it."

With Londoners becoming more focused on healthy eating, is the mighty pud losing favor? "Pudding is still popular," Dias says as people are watching their weight, "but not as popular as it used to be just a few years ago." He continues hopefully, "but it is nice to have a good and caloric pudding once and then...I love haggis," Dias says. "It was love at first sight." Haggis, for the uninitiated, is a Scottish savory pudding containing sheep's heart, liver, and lungs, mixed with beef or mutton fat and oatmeal, and seasoned with onions and spices before it is encased in a sheep's stomach. There's no sheep lung in a jam roly-poly though. There's no blood in a crumble, or a blancmange or a trifle. How did bloody offal turn into a sweet treat? How did puddings veer so far in two different directions, the savories and the sweets?

English pudding has a good and rich history. It is long and varied from the early days of sausages in dark, medieval times—blood puddings, haggis, steak and kidneys—to the other end of the spectrum, the sweet puds—treacle tarts, sticky toffee pudding, and sweet pies. "Éclairs, obviously!" enthuses Jeremie Vaislic, co-founder and CEO of Maître Choux, about his favorite pudding, which is traditionally associated with French cuisine, rather than English. The patisserie's website states that Maître Choux is the first and only choux pastry-specialized patisserie in the world. Says Vaislic, "They're so versatile. Each of them is, really, an individual dessert."

In the earliest days of pudding, the English prepared them to make the offal of animals palatable. There would be no wasting of any part of an animal. Any sort of nourishment was better than none; better to get vitamins from a gut than not having anything in your gut. The early cooking of what would become puddings involved filling intestines and bladders with meat and spices and then boiling them. The word pudding is derived from the French word *boudin*, which, in turn, came from the Latin *bollutus* (sausage or small intestine). Puddings are a British invention developed from the sausages that were brought by the Romans in the 1st century BC.

By the 16th century, puddings were included in cookbooks. Thomas Dalton's *The Good Housewife's Jewel*, published in 1596, offered pudding recipes like black pudding (a blood sausage that was being made as early as the 15th century; one recipe even asked for porpoise blood), haggis (recipes date back to 1430), and "pudding of a calves chaldron" (minced tripe with marrow, spices, and more).

From the late 16th and early 17th centuries came recipes for funeral puddings made from myrtle berries called *murtatum*, as well as "figgy" puddings. Soon, sweeter Christmas puddings made their way to the feast table. "Oh, a wonderful pudding! Bob Cratchit said," wrote Charles Dickens in *A Christmas Carol*, "and calmly too, that he regarded it as the greatest success achieved by Mrs.

Yorkshire Puddings

Black Pudding

Spotted Dick

Jam Roly Poly

Christmas Pudding

Eton Mess

Cratchit since their marriage." White puddings came into fashion (a sibling of the black pudding, but without the blood) too. A 1588 recipe collection featured one white pudding made of beef suet (the raw hard fat of beef or mutton), bread crumbs, egg yolk, and currants, flavored with nutmeg, cinnamon, and sugar.

Myth has it that the Pudding King, as King George I was called, requested plum pudding to be served as part of his royal feast in his first Christmas in England. (The name "Christmas pudding" was first referred to in Eliza Acton's bestselling 1845 cookbook, *Modern Cookery for Private Families*.) In the time of the Pudding King, advances were being made in meat preserving techniques and, at the same time, the cost of sugars and spices were going down so that it was even affordable to the working classes.

There were now two lines of puds—savories and sweets—and sometimes both. These days it's hard to say what constitutes a true pudding because there are now so many varieties. Anything boiled or steamed in a basin, cloth, or bit of an intestinal tract can be considered a pudding. But then there's the Yorkshire pudding, a dish that catches fat dripping from fire-roasting meat and incorporates it into the batter. And then there are sticky toffee puddings, Eve's pudding (apples baked under a sponge cake), bread and butter pudding (also baked). Why are they called puddings at all when they don't adhere to the definition? I have yet to meet a Brit who can answer it outright.

Few puddings captivate quite like the spotted dick. The name alone commands attention. Which brings us to another question: what is the spotted dick? "The Kilburn sisters," noted in the *Pall Mall Gazette* in 1892, "daily [satisfy] hundreds of dockers with soup and spotted dick." It is a pudding made of suet and dried fruit and often served with custard. Dick was another name for pudding in the 19th century. It's possibly the result of an evolving corruption of "pudding" to "puddink," then to "puddick," and finally to just "dick." The spots are the currants that dot the pudding throughout. Giggles abound when a spotted dick is near. There are times in which the spotted dick was renamed spotted Richard by those who didn't want to suffer the inevitable giggles that come with the original name. As one can imagine, that name didn't quite catch on.

Cervantes wrote in *Don Quixote*, "The proof of the pudding is in the eating." Bakewell pudding, apple hat, flummery, Royal Coburg, the Herodotus pud. Puddings after puddings after puddings—Empress pudding, the Barbary, the sweet macaroni, the ginger parkin. "These homey puds are certainly not fine patisserie," noted celebrity chef Hugh Fearnley-Whittingstall in a piece he wrote for *The Guardian*. "They're designed not to seduce the eye so much as to have rural rumpy-pumpy with your tastebuds."

Tastebuds continue to be delighted. "A perfect pudding is the one that makes you think about it," Dias states. "Drives your mind to think on how everything came together." A pudding that "makes you stop talking and start thinking." Vaislic echoes these sentiments. "It's always a good thing to improve on traditional recipes in terms of both flavors and designs." He continues, "The best chefs know how to do this. The most important thing is to deliver on what customers expect to receive." Sometimes that's a haggis. Sometimes it's a spotted dick.

–

Drinking Like The Dickens: The Historic Pubs of London

Words by Jonathan Shipley
Photography by Daniela Velasco

Places to imbibe came by way of the invading Romans. They brought booze and kept them in tabernae, shops that sold wine and quenched the thirsts of troops. While Romans liked wine, the English preferred ale. So, tabernae soon adapted to the local clientele, and beer poured forth from tabernae from then on (the word "tavern" is a corruption of the term "tabernae"). They became so popular that by 1309, in the City of London, there were 354 taverns and an estimated 1,334 brewhouses.

By the end of the 16th century, there were 17,000 ale houses, 2,000 inns, and 400 taverns in England and Wales. Collectively, these public houses became known as "pubs" during the reign of King Henry VII, who sought to regulate them by passing an act in 1552 that required innkeepers to have a license to run a "pub."

Today, drinkers can enjoy a frosty mug at some of the oldest pubs in England:

THE GEORGE INN

In 1475, while the Burgundian Wars were raging, and Londoners were drinking, Thomas Dewe was named owner of the George Inn, a public house located in Southwark, London, not a stone's throw from the River Thames and London Bridge. Although it has been rebuilt twice—after it burned to the ground in 1670, and again in 1676—the George Inn still exists today. You can now sit in the very place where Shakespeare sat, drink where he drank, and wax poetic, half-drunken, like the bard must have done. Shakespeare wrote here in the Elizabethan era, when the tavern was used for theatrical plays.

Centuries later, Charles Dickens liked drinking there so much that he referred to it in his work, *Little Dorrit.* Considered a national treasure, the George Inn is now owned by the National Trust: the only surviving, galleried London coaching inn, traditionally a resting place for people and their horses.

1676
THE GEORGE
THE PROPERTY O
NATIONA
TRUST
GALLERY BAR

THE SPANIARDS INN

Lift a Hammersmith punter here in 2019 knowing that someone lifted a punter in the same pub in 1618. It is believed that this building dates to 1585, once forming the entrance to the estate of the Bishop of London.

The interior is warm, inviting, and dignified. Wood-paneled, with touches of contemporary flair, The Spaniard Inn conveys tradition with an open fire, leather chairs, and cozy corners. In the early days of the inn, highwaymen frequented it. A tree outside the place (now removed) was used to hang ne'er-do-wells. The pub was mentioned in Dickens' *The Pickwick Papers*, and Bram Stoker's *Dracula* as well. Byron drank here. John Keats too, who wrote "Ode to a Nightingale" in the inn's garden.

YE OLDE CHESHIRE CHEESE

There has been a pub where Ye Olde Cheshire Cheese stands since 1585 (by the front door is a list of every monarch of England who has reigned since). Rebuilt after the Great London Fire in 1666, the pub is now located down a narrow alleyway. Each of the pub's rooms has a different style. With no natural light, the pub's fireplaces are often lit during the cold months. A vaulted cellar dates back to the 13th century, when a Carmelite monastery stood on the site.

Notable visitors have included Mark Twain; Alfred, Lord Tennyson; Sir Arthur Conan Doyle; P.G. Wodehouse; Samuel Johnson; and, as you might have guessed, Charles Dickens, who mentioned this pub in *A Tale of Two Cities*. Also, a parrot named Polly lived in the pub for nearly 40 years. When Polly died in 1926, her obituary appeared in 200 newspapers around the world.

Located on Fleet Street (yes, the same street of the fictitious demon barber Sweeney Todd), Ye Olde Cheshire Cheese serves pub favorites like bangers and mash, ploughman's lunches, and Scotch eggs.

THE PROSPECT AT WHITBY

This is the oldest riverside tavern in London. Dating to around 1520, the oldest remnants of its early days is the 400-year-old stone floor. The pub was so dark (and can still be, depending on London's gray weather) that it was called the Devil's Tavern. Reprobates frequented the place—swindlers and cut throats, smugglers and thieves.

Writers like Dickens and the diarist Samuel Pepys drank here. But so did artists, like J.M.W. Turner, who sketched views from this pub's windows, and James A.M. Whistler, whose painting of his mother (not painted inside of the pub) is now one of the most recognizable images ever created.

Today, The Prospect at Whitby serves fresh pub food, like steak and red wine pie, mushroom pudding, and house-made sausages. Drinks include ales from its Suffolk brewery.

THE LAMB AND FLAG

Along with Dickens, bare-knuckle boxers drank at The Lamb and Flag, a rough-and-tumble pub in the previously rough-and-tumble neighborhood of Covent Garden. Upstairs, the bare-knuckled toughs fought so much the place was nicknamed The Bucket of Blood.
Today, people fight for a table to eat good food and drink good drinks. The menu includes salt and pepper squid, smoked haddock, goat cheese tarts, Eton mess, and beer.

–

GUINNESS
SIX NATIONS

WELCOME TO THE
GEORGE INN
IN SOUTHWARK
Est. 1542
PERVEYORS of
SPIRITS & WINES
BEERS & ALES

Verbal Indigestion: A Guide to Cockney Rhyming Slang

Words and photography by
Aaron Bernstein and Isabel Lea

Food and language have always been playfully interwoven, but this is especially true in the pubs, markets, and social venues of London. When you grow up in England today, you might be told not to tell "porky pies"—a rhyming synonym for "lies." These strange rhyming substitutions can seem puzzling to foreigners—especially as there are only a few examples used now in day-to-day British English. However, in the heart of East London in the 1850s and 1900s, it wouldn't have been uncommon to hear requests for a "pig's ear" or a "Vera Lynn" as a way of asking for "beer" or "gin," respectively. These days, Cockney rhyming slang exists mostly satirised in TV shows and in few surviving phrases such as "porky pies." However, scratching beneath the surface reveals an East London dialect built on an abundance of playful food metaphors.

Cockney rhyming slang was the spoken dialect of the Cockney. Historically, "Cockney" itself was a slang term referring to working class inhabitants of East London, one of the poorest areas in Victorian England. In fact, the word for Cockney itself comes from "misshapen egg"—an insult to people born and raised in this area. The language has its origins in the Victorian period (1837-1901), an era of great industrialisation and an accompanying wealth and class division. As a result, there were also growing differences in the lifestyles and dialects of the area's communities. Some sources believe that Cockney rhyming slang emerged from these converging forces. Whether it was used to maintain a sense of community within East London or simply to exclude and confuse outsiders is unclear. The dialect, affectionately referred to by expert Peter Wright as a form of "verbal indigestion" because of the difficulty in "digesting" the coded rhymes, might substitute "apple and pears" for "stairs"—"I took a tumble down the apple and pears."

Within the origin debate, some scholars theorise that it began as a secret language among beggars, while others maintain it started as an underhand communication system for thieves (or "tea leaves"). Additional origin theories suggest that

VHF
UHF
SOLID STATE

it was born as an amusing set of verbal riddles from bricklayers, or that Cockney labourers and engineers used it to confuse rival Irish construction gangs. While the origins are hotly debated, it's acknowledged widely that the dialect developed most in the pubs and informal social spaces of East London. As a result, any, or a combination of these, could have been the starting point, with its usage accelerated by different communities mixing, talking, overhearing, and adopting different phrases. The beauty of the rhyming slang is that it adapted and grew, taking on a life of its own. In fact, to this day, variations of Cockney rhyming slang are found as far away as the U.S. and Australia.

As a spoken dialect, it's very hard to classify rhyming slang, or even write it out phonetically. Surprisingly, when written, some rhyming slang doesn't appear to rhyme at all. This is due to the fact that the cockney "i" sounds more like "oi." The best rhymes, however, have a literal meaning and rhyming counterparts that cleverly relate to each other.

Often, when foods are used in the rhyme, they are not the ones commonly used in day-to-day speech, so as not to be confused with the literal meaning. This gives interesting insight about the food habits at this time for the working class. An example of this is "mince pies," which is used as rhyming slang for "eyes." Given that you'd seldom be complaining about a problem with your actual mince pies, the meaning tends to remain clear because of context. Sometimes, however, the relationship can be metaphorical, such as "satin and silk" meaning "milk" because of the related appearance. Some phrases, on the other hand, are more conceptually related; to ask about "bread and honey," for example, would mean to be asking about "money." People and public figures are also a popular subject for the rhymes, with "baked bean" being a synonym for "queen."

Due to being a spoken dialect often accompanied by a pint or two, there is often a level of social commentary or amusing absurdity to the phrases. For example, aside from "custard and jelly" meaning the popular British dessert, its Cockney rhyming slang refers to a "telly." Some phrases like this one have no clear correlation at all, but do pose an interesting mental image.

The dialect was born out of the hardships of East London life. Simple objects and words were used playfully, and they reflected the culture of and relationship that the Cockney people had with work, leisure, food, and drink. The important thing in the dialect is not the rules, but the way the word choice and sentiment reflects culture. While the dialect in its purest form is no longer commonly spoken, some of the food-related language is still integrated into common usage, like "porky pies" (i.e., "lies"). To this day, if you put on your "ones and twos" ("shoes") and head down to certain parts of East London, you might still be able to sample a serving of Cockney rhyming slang with your "pig's ear" ("beer").

–

The Life and Times of the Great British Pie

Words by John Surico
Photography by Adam Goldberg and Daniela Velasco

When you think of your standard British pie, you might imagine eating it in a place like Rules, the oldest restaurant in London. With dimmed lights and English banter, this eatery on Maiden Lane in London's posh Covent Garden neighborhood has been serving what it calls "traditional British food" since 1798. In the way of pies, that means steak and kidney pie, steamed steak and kidney suet pie, and fish pie, with smoked haddock as the *poisson du jour*.

And you wouldn't necessarily be incorrect. Ever since it was developed in 12th century Northern Europe, when olive oil was hard to come by and fishermen needed small meals that could store well and still taste great on long sails, the British pie has been exactly that: traditional. Be it savory or sweet—but more likely savory; Britons will tell you: Americans are the experts on sweet pies—meat pies of pastry and puff are a cornerstone of cuisine here. You can find them at any restaurant like Rules, and practically everywhere else in the United Kingdom: in pubs and classic "pie and mash" shops; in home kitchens and at holiday dinners; in "Sweeney Todd;" and the frozen sections of Tesco's and Sainsbury's.

So when Rakesh Singh helped open Cinnamon Bazaar, an Indian-fusion restaurant just a few doors down from Rules, that's what he thought about. The British pie was a dish everyone living in London recognizes. So what could he possibly add? "We wanted to cook something familiar," Chef Singh said, on a recent visit to the restaurant. He then pondered a question at the heart of what drives culinary change: "What could we do for the British people to like it?"

The result is a symbol of what modern-day London looks like: the lamb *rogan josh* shepherd's pie, defined by its distinct flavors of cardamom, masala, onion, curry, and garlic. It has the familiar heartiness of a British shepherd's pie, with peas and buttery mash, but is taken up a few notches in spice with cumin.

"I knew that pies were such a focus here, and lamb *rogan josh* is so popular where

HE PIE
ROOM
THE
ROO

I'm from in India," he added. "So what could be new there?" Singh was clearly onto something: the pie was rated by Time Out as one of London's 100 best dishes, and has quickly become a hit at the restaurant, where about 100 pies are served per week. On a recent visit, our table wasn't the only one with a pie (or two) present.

But Singh isn't the only one thinking about what traditional means in his country's cuisine right now. Across London, a cadre of cooks are redefining what the British pie can be, not coincidentally at a moment when the forces of tradition and change seem to be set on a collision course in the isle kingdom. As the question of Brexit underlies nearly every conversation about London's future, the city is having an identity crisis, and that can be seen in one of its most classic dishes. It is, perhaps, a sign of the times that a stalwart of the British palate, which hadn't really seen much change for centuries, is being ripped from the past, and thrown into the future. And Londoners don't seem to mind at all. In fact, they're hungry for it.

//

When Ravinder Bhogal was growing up in London, Friday nights were what her family called "English food nights." Her parents, who had roots in the Middle East and Africa, would try their hand at British dishes, but keep their own recipes alive—butter was laced with ginger and carrot seeds, and since mangos weren't as fresh, her family made their chutney with Bramley apples. What drives Bhogal's thinking is a simple truth: these remixed recipes tasted *better*.

"Immigrant recipes are never over. When you mix your old culinary heritage with new ingredients, you make your own cuisine," she told me, when the two of us met at her bright, colorful restaurant Jikoni in Marylebone. "You can ask how you can make it 'authentic,' but it's your landscape, your story. That's what makes it authentic."

Her words rang true as we dissected her renowned scrag end pie, which comes out in a hot clay dish after it's baked at a low temperature for 24 hours. Scrag end, she explained, is a cut taken from a lamb's neck, where it's more gelatinous and fattier. In every bite, you didn't just taste the turmeric—you were confronted by it. That, and ginger, chiles, garlic, and cinnamon, with a soft mash topping, for good measure. "It's essentially a shepherd's pie, but one that transcends cultural boundaries and heritages," she said. "So you're hit with the flavor that you always knew, and then you're hit with all these pops of new flavors."

It's that sensation that for Bhogal—who is now an acclaimed chef, TV host, and author—brings joy to people. Food has this incredible power to transport; just one bite can whisk us away to another time and place entirely, when we remember these flavors, and could almost see those memories play out in film reel format—be it a birthday meal with your parents as a child; a first date; or a visit to see family members from afar for the holidays.

For so many Britons, she said, the pie has a firm grip on that nostalgia. So it's no surprise that pies are back in the spotlight, she argues, what with a vote to leave the European Union looming and populism challenging certain notions of liberal democracy; in times like these, says Bhogal, we willingly seek out those feelings of nostalgia and reassurance. And increasingly, we're doing that through what we eat. "Everyone is feeling very overwhelmed," Bhogal explained. "In worrying times, people want comfort."

When Marco Casadei opened up Young Vegans Pie Shop at Camden Market with his wife, Carla, after a number of street cart stints, they took a gamble on what Britons would digest—they made the meat pie entirely vegan. Steak, lamb, and chicken were replaced with seitan; vegan cheese swapped in for dairy cheese; and gravy went plant-based. And like any good vegan alternative, it's not that you can't taste the difference; you're not even trying to.

"We wanted to make a traditional meal, but we didn't want to do traditional," Casadei, a native Londoner, told me,

Chicken, Girolle, & Tarragon Pie, The Pie Room.

THE PIE ROOM
HOLBORN
DINING ROOM
FROM THE OVEN

as we grabbed a pint nearby the shop. "Because that's boring, and frankly, we didn't like those tastes. We're not tied to that tradition. We can make our own."

The response has been overwhelming. What started out as a pie-making operation in their apartment has launched into a full-on prep kitchen, wholesale aspirations, and a vegan pizza shop (Death by Pizza) on the other side of London, with plenty of meat-eaters stopping by to try out the new takes. Customers, he said, are returning to the idea that the British pie could be this *tabula rasa* of taste, he argued, after years of seeing it mass produced. "People just lost interest," he recounted. "It was so cheap, and so basic. It was no longer this sought-after dish."

Looking back, Casadei said that vegan pies had all the ingredients for success right now. Not only did you have the longing for comfort food, but also, concern over rising carbon emissions has forced many consumers to rethink their lifestyles. And at a time when people perceive going out to eat as another form of entertainment—something they're willing to spend a significant portion of their money on—then that extends naturally to food. "It was almost inevitable that plant-based culture was going to take off," he said.

//

Before I left London, I was told by several people that I couldn't write a story on British pies without consulting Calum Franklin, the executive chef at the Holborn Dining Room. Just as Singh and Bhogal had brought in regional flavors, and Casadei, a meat-free alternative, Franklin has become a celebrity of sorts—at least in the food Instagram world—for hand-crafting beautiful British pies. And he has made it his mission to give the age-old dish new life.

That interest was first sparked four years ago, when Franklin found an old pie mold in the basement of the dining room. He asked a number of chefs he knew how to use it, and none of them could respond. "I just realized that there were massive gaps in my knowledge of our own culture," said Franklin, who grew up in Britain. "This was being forgotten."

Franklin spent the next seven months researching recipes at the British Library, and unearthing early photographs of pie rooms, which, in the Victorian era, were often attached to pubs. He said that many kitchens had abandoned the art years ago because pie-making requires heavy manual labor, and is time-consuming. In their place came either mass-produced pies that weren't of the same quality, he said, or pie and mash shops with liquor (or parsley sauce), which, like American diners, have seen their appeal slow amongst younger generations.

He designed a partial space of the brasserie after the 19th-century model, covering the walls in wooden shelves and aged kitchenware, with a center table and ovens for baking and cooking. The space could be easily seen by the public, with a window on the street—"The Pie Hole"—where customers could purchase small pies. Chefs were then invited from all over the world to come learn the art of pie-making. Thus, the Pie Room was born.

"We wanted to save something that was quintessentially British," he said. "It was a part of our history."

In the square kitchen, Franklin showed me some recent creations: curry pies; a pie modeled off of a coin found in the Thames, and had originated in an area nearby; and kidney pies, with a thin, doughy crust. It is an effort, Franklin continued, to regain that institutional knowledge about the timeless classic, and reinvent British cuisine for the better. And it should come as no surprise then that out of the 35 chef-invitees who frequent the room, only three are British in birth: if the pie is to serve up slices of identity for Londoners, then it must get with the times.

"We want to show people that British cuisine isn't just fish and chips," Franklin told me, next to his sketches and recipes. "If I can use this very room to do just that, then that's great."

–

On Sunday, We Roast

Words by Sarah Kollmorgen
Photography by Daniela Velasco

When mighty Roast Beef was the Englishman's food,
It ennobled our veins and enriched our blood.
Our soldiers were brave and our courtiers were good
Oh! the Roast Beef of old England,
And old English Roast Beef!

Henry Fielding wrote this popular ballad, appropriately titled "Roast Beef of Old England," in 1731 as an ode to the great powers of roast beef to make Englishmen "robust, stout, and strong." However, roast beef has never really ceased to be the Englishman's food. Even today, the British perform an ode to roast beef nearly each week in the form of the Sunday roast.

Commonly comprised of roast beef, potatoes, vegetables, and gravy, the Sunday roast, also known as Sunday lunch, remains a foundation of the British culinary world. For many, it's an occasion to bring together family and loved ones for the afternoon, and show off recipes that have been passed down generation by generation. Even in today's fast-paced, convenience-first world, local pubs and restaurants are increasingly focusing their Sunday menus on family-style roast selections, rather than trendy breakfast fads. Although much has changed since 1731, the English love for a meal of roast beef apparently hasn't—and maybe never will.

//

As with most cultural traditions, the precise origins of the British Sunday roast are tangled amidst fact and folklore. Some historical accounts attribute the creation of the beef-centered meal to King Henry VII, who fed his soldiers so much beef weekly after church services that they were dubbed "beefeaters."

Martha Overeynder, a student at Oxford Brookes University writing a dissertation on the cultural and social history of roast beef in Great Britain in the last two centuries, believes that key points in the history of the development of the Sunday roast coincide with times when meat became available to a broader social spectrum, such as during the Industrial Revolution when more families saw an expendable income and could afford luxuries such as meat.

"An extreme example of this is within the workhouses of the 19th century," she says. "During the week, the meals given to the workers would have been measly and not very high in nutritional value. If you think about the depiction of Oliver Twist's infamous gruel, then you will get the picture. However, on a Sunday evening, the workers within the workhouse were given a more substantial meal."

Because roasts are both time-intensive and expensive, Overeynder says people often saved roasts for special occasions, such as a Sunday or holiday. It wasn't until the mid-20th century, when poultry farming became more economical, that chicken and turkey began replacing beef among mid- to low-income families.

From her preliminary research, Overeynder hypothesizes that one factor that makes the Sunday roast particularly British in nature is the meat's connection to the day of rest, restoring your body, eating well, and being with loved ones before the week ahead. In fact, for many English today it seems that more important than the food itself is perhaps the small traditions they've developed to make the Sunday roast their own.

//

For Suzie Normanton, a resident of the small market town of Haslemere in Surrey, the best part of the Sunday roast is the preparation. She starts on the meat and vegetables early Sunday with her husband.

"We listen to a [BBC] Radio 2 program called Steve Wright's *Sunday Love Songs* from 9 am to 10:30 am," she says. "It's the perfect amount of time and background for the preparation of a family roast dinner."

Today, the traditional Sunday lunch consists of a hearty main meat, such as beef, chicken or lamb; a variety or roasted vegetables like carrots or parsnips; roast potatoes; Yorkshire pudding; and a flood of gravy.

Roast Hereford & Yorkshire Pudding, Marksman.

Normanton, however, tends to forgo more classic roasts for more diverse options, such as roast chicken accompanied by roast potatoes cooked with chipolata sausages, roast sweet potatoes, and roast parsnips, as well as a selection of vegetables served in one big bowl. She usually serves a Sunday roast in the late autumn and winter later in the evening for herself, her husband, and her son: "With the darker nights, it makes us feel cosy and hunkered up, and they go well with red wine and a real fire."

Christine Taylor, who currently lives on the Channel Island of Jersey, fondly remembers Sunday roasts with her family while growing up in Ipswich in Suffolk. Yorkshire pudding became a requirement with any meat, she says, because she and her brother loved them so much.

"They were just great family times," she says. "We ate dinner together every day, but on a Sunday for a roast dinner we would set up the dining table, so it always felt special. It was never rushed. It was time to enjoy quality family time and good food."

Although Taylor doesn't cook roasts as often, she still enjoys the meal whenever visiting her parents.

The Sunday Roast is all about hospitality for Sheena Tresidder and her family. Tresidder lives in the quiet London neighborhood of Hampstead and works as a full-time housewife, foster care mother, and pastor's wife. Today, she hosts a Sunday roast every week for her family, friends, and members of their church—a mix of singles, couples, families, and children.

"We are Christian and want to model what we hope our church family is doing," Tresidder says. "We try and invite new people fairly quickly to make them feel comfortable, to get to know them better, to bring them into our home and offer them hospitality—just to begin building a relationship with them."

No meal is complete without Tresidder's gravy, which contains a secret mix of hoisin and sticky plum sauces. Even Brits holding fast to tradition adapt and introduce flavors from cultures all over the world into the Sunday roast.

//

Despite its close ties to the home, the Sunday lunch is increasingly appearing on pub and restaurant menus throughout the United Kingdom. A cursory Google search turns up a large number of "best Sunday roast" lists for different cities, vegan and vegetarian palates, and even those looking for "quirky" roasts.

Sally Abe, head chef at the Michelin-starred pub Harwood Arms in London, attributes today's urban, convenience-first culture with the proliferation of special Sunday lunch menus."People will always cook a roast at home," she says. "But I think in London a lot of people don't have the time or the peace, so it is nice to be able to offer a friendly atmosphere in which they can enjoy a roast all the same."

Chefs Jon Rotheram and Tom Harris from the Marksman, the first public house in all of London to be awarded the Michelin Pub of the Year, offered a similar analysis.

"We thought very carefully what people expect of Sunday roasts, being how your nan would roast potatoes, or your mum's Yorkshire puddings," says Harris. "It's very hard competing with those expectations."

For that reason, Harris and Rotheram say they try and create a friendly, homey atmosphere on Sundays. Like the Harwood Arms and many other restaurants, the Marksman forgoes one-course meals on Sunday in favor of larger, family-style offerings.

Aurelien Durand, general manager at The Admiral Codrington, a traditional pub in London, says he has also noticed people going out with family and friends to enjoy a Sunday roast—especially in the city. In conjunction with this trend, Durand notes that he's also seen an improvement in the quality of Sunday roast over the past decade.

This can certainly be seen in the menus of pubs and restaurants throughout England. At The Admiral Codrington, roast vegetables are sometimes cooked, steamed, and finished with a mixture of orange juice and honey. On Marksman's Sunday menu, you can find Braised Oxtail & Dumplings, as well as Marmalade Steamed Pudding. The Harwood Arms prides itself on using beef that's been dry-aged for 45 days.

The best part of a Sunday lunch on the town however? "You don't have to wash up," Abe says.

Just as Sunday will always be part of the seven-day week, it seems that the Sunday roast will remain a part of British life. The sides and ingredients may change to match the culinary trends of the times, and its significance may always be slightly different for different people. However, its core components seem likely to stay the same: Good food, good company, and good conversation.

–

Roast Hereford & Yorkshire Pudding, Buttered Greens, Roast Potatoes & Sage, Marksman.

2016
BOULEVARD

The Tastes of Wimbledon

Words by Neha Pearce
Illustration by Monique Aimee

Juicy strawberries bathed in fresh cream, an invigorating pitcher of Pimm's No.1 redolent of spiced citrus, and the top tennis talent in the world. This can only mean Wimbledon. There's no guarantee of sun, but summertime has arrived in the British Isles.

"The Championships, Wimbledon," often referred to simply as "Wimbledon," is a tennis tournament steeped in tradition. The All England Lawn Tennis and Croquet Club has hosted the event since 1877, when a modest 200 attendees watched 20 men compete in a singles competition. It is the only one of the four Grand Slams (also known as "majors," they are comprised of Roland-Garros, also known as the French Open; the U.S. Open; the Australian Open; and Wimbledon) that is still played on grass, just like the aristocrats played "lawn tennis" in Victorian times. In many respects, Wimbledon tries to preserve its tradition of civility for the best experience for all. Competitors are still addressed as "ladies" and "gentlemen" and required to dress in all-white or face disqualification. And the tournament tries to limit advertisement at a loss of revenue and still closes its courts to matches on Sundays to respect the peace and quiet of its hosting town of Wimbledon.

Just a 30-minute Tube journey from the center of London, 15,000 people stream into the verdant suburb of Wimbledon for two weeks each year to witness tennis history in action. Although ticket prices range from £60 to £50,000, and despite its aristocratic undertones, Wimbledon makes an effort to make attendance possible for everyone by providing a lottery system and reserving a percentage of low-cost, same-day tickets for those who are willing to stand in the infamous 24-hour queue.

The food at the tournament represents Wimbledon's dedication to sharing British heritage with both high society and fans who travel from around the world to have a taste. Strawberries and cream, as an example, have been an icon since the first tournament, when strawberries happened to be in style among the upper class. The sweet rubies at Wimbledon are hulled, inspected, and served with airy mounds of sweet, soft-peaked double cream. Hugh Lowe Farms, a 120-year-old, family-owned berry farm over 30 miles away in Kent, has supplied all of Wimbledon's strawberries for the last 25 years. Every day of the tournament, at 4 a.m., the workers of Hugh Lowe Farms awake to pick the berries that have been specifically grown to reach ripeness during match play. For those doubtful that the tournament's signature snack could be anything special, look no further than the 1.4 million strawberries Wimbledon viewers consume each year. And that's not including the keychains, magnets, and towels sold at various kiosks on tournament grounds to commemorate visitors' love for the tasty tradition.

Just as equivalent to summer in England is Pimm's Cup No. 1. This breezy gin spirit, served with mint and as many fresh fruits as possible, has been the drink of Wimbledon since its inception. Pimm's itself was created by a London oyster bar owner in the 1840s and sold as digestive relief, but soon grew in popularity. It is one of Wimbledon's seven, carefully chosen and official food and drink partners.

The Wimbledon grounds contain 49 on-site kitchens, 27 restaurants, and 29 grab-and-go stations, not to mention the popular backpack picnics available for pick-up. All of these are overseen by a total of 355 chefs who are dedicated to upholding the dignity of Wimbledon by sourcing sustainable ingredients that showcase the best of British produce.

Other traditional foods enjoyed by attendees, as well as fans who recreate the experience on their own at home, are afternoon tea and coronation chicken sandwiches. High tea encourages guests to relax, as they try to eat as many fresh baked scones with jam and clotted cream as possible. Wimbledon's scones are made by the The Cake Store, a family-owned bakery in London that works in overdrive during the tournament, cranking out 10,000 scones a day.

The coronation chicken sandwich, though often woefully represented these days as a soggy convenience store sandwich, was created for Queen Elizabeth II's coronation by the principals of the French culinary school, Le Cordon Bleu. This sweet and creamy poached chicken sandwich, bound with a curried mayonnaise dressing, was invented to be fit for royalty, but austere enough for those post-WWII days of rationing.

Wimbledon began 125 years ago as a small summer pastime for a private tennis club, but it has since grown into the one of the world's most distinguished tennis tournaments. Today, the foods that have sustained its visitors and players for over a century are as iconic as the all-white dress code, carrying British heritage, tradition, and history in every bite.

–

No1
PIMM'S

Courtside

As told to Daniela Velasco
Illustration by Aiste Stancikaite

The only common thread on match day for Wimbledon players and attendees is that they are all clad in white. Athletes gearing up for major matches at the tournament are less inclined to partake in the free flow of Pimm's or abundant strawberries and cream that have made food and beverage at Wimbledon famous. Just ask Heather Watson, the friendly British 26-year-old ranked as one of the top 50 doubles players in the world and in the top 100 in singles play. Below, we go courtside with the Brit at her home tournament to see how she prepares for high-pressure matches on the iconic lawns of Wimbledon.

How do you prepare eating-wise before a tennis match? Does it vary depending on where you are—for example, at Wimbledon versus, say, the U.S. Open? It does vary depending on where I am because of what is available and also what I feel like, but it would usually be a small meal with carbs like rice or pasta. I don't like plain food, so I would usually add some protein and vegetables to it. I hate feeling full on court, so I would rather eat too little than too much.

Have you tried the food at Wimbledon? Do you have any favorite restaurants or dishes at the tournament? All of the Grand Slams have amazing food choices, so I eat all of my meals on the grounds when I am onsite. Wimbledon always has amazing salmon in the restaurant, so I usually get that. They also seem to have an endless supply of strawberries and cream.

Are strawberries and cream really the most quintessential British courtside snack? Yes, they are. Also Pimm's is a very popular drink to have on court in the summer. They've become real trademarks of The Championships and make it sort of an *experience*. It is sort of like having a hot dog in New York; it just has to be done.

Can you walk us through a match day at Wimbledon? Pre-game, during game, and post-game? Wake up, have breakfast, do a physical warm-up for around 30 minutes, and then immediately do a tennis warm-up for around 30 minutes. Then I'll shower and change into match clothes. Then wait for my match in a quiet place and maybe eat again if there is a lot of time. After that, I play my match and hopefully win! Then shower, media, stretch, ice bath, and I'll end with a massage.

How, if at all, does Wimbledon's reputation affect your matchplay there? Wimbledon is the [tennis] tournament with the most history and traditions. That makes it so special to be a part of and play at. Also, being my home Grand Slam makes it extra special. I can't speak for everyone, but I think Wimbledon is the Slam that players want to win the most.

What catered food do they provide for the athletes? They have a main players' restaurant and another one at the practice courts. The food is brilliant and you pretty much have everything: hot food, pasta bar, salad bar, sandwiches, drinks, snacks, coffee, smoothies, and the list goes on.

After all of the matches are played, where do you go out to eat and drink? Where are the spots where you know you'll run into the other tennis players? During Wimbledon, for the last seven years, I have stayed with a host family that lives right by Wimbledon. We are now such close family friends, and even though I have my own home in London, I still choose to stay with them, as I love it there. The mother is a chef, so I've never eaten out in Wimbledon during The Championships, because her food is to die for.

What's the one snack that you can't live without? Little easy-peel oranges, as they're healthy and delicious.

What food do you get excited to eat/drink while in London? I mostly just drink water, but the food I get most excited about in London would have to be Asian fusion. There are so many restaurants in London with incredible food, so it is hard to pick just one; but if I had to, it would be the volcano roll at Dozo in Soho.

–

Refraction

Words by James Hansen
Photography by Maureen M. Evans

Ask chefs and restaurant folks around the world to recommend a place in London, and they'll probably direct you to St. John. Fergus Henderson and Trevor Gulliver's restaurant in Smithfield, a few steps from the area's eponymous meat market, has become a local and global icon for its unique approach to cooking, as much as it is a storied dining room.

Michelin-starred, globally adored, and long-established, St. John and its lineage of graduating chefs have taken its ethos and refracted it through a changing city of growing dining renown and increasing diversity.

//

The restaurant's logo is an anatomical drawing of a whole, nose-to-tail pig. But it's not just a cipher. At St. John, they serve the real thing: a whole pig's head on a platter—the soft fold of the crisped ear, the puff of the jiggling cheeks puckering in at the snout. No amount of accompanying lentils, simmered down into a soothing brown stew, or green salad bitter with endive, sharp with lemon, and hoarse with the croak of shallot, can tell a diner another story about what they are eating. This is the emblem of a city's most influential restaurant: the whitewashed Clerkenwell shrine to British cooking that did for London what Noma helped do for Copenhagen.

St. John restored London's pride in its own English food, which had been stamped out by the terror of World War II and ration coupons decades before. Opened in 1994, the restaurant's 25 years on Smithfield are a dateline for London's maturation as a restaurant city, an indicator that London food had finally unshackled itself from fusty adherence to French classicism. Still, though: one of St, John's most adored dishes is simply a plate of warm madeleines. Food is never that straightforward.

In 2019, St. John is more institution than iconoclast. The original location at Smithfield has held a Michelin star since 2009, and has become a symbol of quality for many, and a symbol of starched

Chef Fergus Henderson.

Rum & Raisin Parfait, St. John.

WINE
SALES

tablecloth-stuffiness for a great many too. Its sister restaurant, St. John Bread and Wine, opposite the commuter-hipster thrum of Spitalfields Market, is probably the more interesting restaurant today, its envelope pushed a little further.

Henderson's book, *The Complete Nose-to-Tail*, a compilation of recipes from both restaurants is given to each and every chef that passes through the Spitalfields kitchen. The chef must choose a recipe to read, dissect, and cook with Henderson, mindful of the recipe's quirks of taste and meaning. The chef then takes ownership of that recipe, passing the insight on to others in the kitchen before the dish is served. It's that blend of autonomy and camaraderie that makes St. John's influence on London most interesting when explored through the chefs who graduate the kitchen—the paths they take, the traditions they invoke and create, with echoes of St. John tolling the way.

LEE TIERNAN, BLACK AXE MANGAL

Lee Tiernan spent 11 years at St. John Bread and Wine. His restaurant Black Axe Mangal is very different from St. John. But the two restaurants are in a dialogue.

Black Axe Mangal is a collision, not a fusion or an assimilation. A signature dish, lamb offal flatbread, is Fergus Henderson's nose-to-tail ethos smashed against the Istanbul *ocakbaşı* ("fireside," referring to charcoal barbecue) and *mangal* grill culture that winds its way through Dalston, Green Lanes, Newington Green, and Edmonton—the areas where Turkish and Kurdish communities settled. Snarling with cumin, garlic, and the heat of the grill, the meat paste is pounded into a fresh-baked flatbread, covered in a tangle of sumac onions, chiles, and parsley. Nodding to the *lahmacuns* (the pizza-like round of thin, baked dough topped with minced meat, vegetables, herbs, and spices) that line so many of this city's streets; to Danny Bowien, whose wing spice features on the menu; and to St. John with offal, bone marrow, and simple terrines on silver platters, Black Axe Mangal is a restaurant so dependent on London's culinary intersections that it likely could not exist anywhere else. And: that "terrine" is a deep-fried pressing of rabbit. It's called "Crispy Fucking Rabbit." You get the idea—Black Axe Mangal is a treasure.

JAMES LOWE, LYLE'S

If Tiernan's Black Axe Mangal is reactionary, Lyle's is a more subtle evolution from St. John's ethos.

Nose-to-tail is not a phrase you'll hear at Lyle's, a gorgeous, whitewashed room in Shoreditch. James Lowe met his co-founder John Ogier at St. John Bread and Wine—Lowe as head chef, and Ogier as general manager. Lowe is particularly vocal about how words like nose-to-tail, farm-to-table, and other similar phrases have been overused to the point of redundancy. Except, perhaps, when talking about St. John.

A hallmark of Lowe's cooking here is game—not just in its eating, but in its seasonality—the inspiration for an international guest series showing the chefs of the world Britain's unique products. The food at Lyle's is rib-sticking and fortifying in the winter; it is lighter, brighter, and spritzier in the summer. And in Anna Higham, it has one of London's most talented pastry chefs. The attention to detail in the kitchen expands to all areas: The bar serves speciality coffee from around the world at a level that would make so many third-wave cafes blush, and a lean, typeset menu changes daily with à la carte dishes at lunch and a set menu at dinner. The grammar of its menu, like St. John's, is pared back. But little touches—the names of vegetables, growers, butchers, and cheeses that would never be found in Henderson's restaurants—are quiet hints to where this magnificent restaurant diverges from its forbear. Lyle's is Lowe, Ogier, and their team's own place, as much as Black Axe Mangal is Tiernan's, and St. John is Henderson's and Gulliver's.

Potted Pork, St. John.

St. JOHN
DOES NOT ACCEPT
ANY RESPONSIBILITY
FOR PERSONAL
BELONGINGS

Eccles Cake & Lancashire Cheese, St. John.

Chef Fergus Henderson.

Lemon Sole, Bread & Capers, St. John Bread and Wine.

Vanilla Cream & Poached Quince, St. John Bread and Wine.

Bacon Sandwich, Rochelle Canteen.

Rochelle Canteen.

MARGOT HENDERSON AND MELANIE ARNOLD, ROCHELLE CANTEEN

The food at St. John so often teeters on the edge of ordinariness—but never quite inhabits it. Pared back simplicity, the way it is employed at St. John, is exposing. Brash adventurousness can often mask a lack of technique or understanding; here, the risk of seeming plain pays off.

Rochelle Canteen is snuck away in a former Shoreditch school bike shed, adjacent to a refuge for immigrants in a hub of London's burgeoning "creative class." In a way, the restaurant is married to St. John, and in another, it is entirely distinct.

Margot and Fergus Henderson opened The French House Dining Room in Soho in 1992 after a courtship involving coriander, cabbage pasta, and close encounters at formica tables. In Soho, working with Jon Spiteri, another industry veteran, they drew in happy crowds. But, in 1994, Fergus opened St. John with Trevor Gulliver. Margot, together with business partner Melanie Arnold—Spiteri's wife, who also helped to run The French House Dining Room—opened Rochelle Canteen a decade later.

Time is the only metric by which Rochelle Canteen is "after" St. John. (And its similarities to Rose Gray's and Ruth Rogers's partnership at The River Café cannot be ignored. Although, that pair was more influenced by Italian cooking.) Rochelle is a little less explicitly British-but-French than St. John. The self-effacing name makes the curt confidence of its menu read with a cheekier wink. But, still, there are no fussy garnishes, no food stacked on top of itself like Jenga pieces. It is "green sauce," not salsa verde at Rochelle Canteen. A whole quail shines next to a splodge of aioli and a big meat pie is served in a big white dish. With distinct identities, but shared DNA, St. John and Rochelle Canteen are part of a family, but their personalities are, necessarily, their own.

–

Modern Briton

Interview by Maggie Spicer
Photography by Adam Goldberg and Daniela Velasco

The airy, canteen-style dining room at Lyle's on East London's Shoreditch High Street is at once familiar and refreshing. With a bright, open kitchen perched behind a neat collection of tables and shaker chairs beneath tall ceilings, Lyle's makes you feel as if you could have just as easily stumbled upon a school lunchroom of generations past or a friend's dinner gathering at a loft apartment.

At its helm is James Lowe, whose experience includes time spent at The Fat Duck and St. John Bread & Wine. On any given afternoon his hands are full, receiving some of the city's (and home counties') best produce, harvested that morning, still glistening with dew.

You first got into cooking at age 23, then proceeded to work at some of London's top restaurants before opening your own by the age of 30. How would you say that drive has manifested at Lyle's since you opened? I opened the restaurant to learn about British produce, discover more producers, and see where we could take the food. The press needed a title for the restaurant. "It's modern British," I would answer. People didn't really know what the food was when we opened. I didn't really know entirely what it meant. But, we would find out and explore what that modern British cuisine meant after we opened.

We change menus on a regular basis. We make sure we don't repeat a dish. I wanted to make this restaurant a London institution. I wanted it to be thought of in the same way as The River Cafe, The Fat Duck, or St. John. I worked at these restaurants because I had a huge amount of respect for them and their chefs. None of these establishments were smash hits from the start. Rather, they evolved over time, always innovating, serving as leaders in what they were doing. And there was a need for what they were doing.

I felt the same for Lyle's. We weren't super busy when we opened and we didn't get great reviews, but I felt what we are doing was needed and valid in London. So, that's how the ambition has come through. I want us to celebrate our 10th birthday, and for the restaurant to be busy—to me, that feels like validation of the reasons why we opened. We serve people nice food at a good value. We're using the same, if not better, produce than what you get at some of the best restaurants in London, yet many are charging double for their menus.

We won our Michelin star in 2015, and entered the World's 50 Best at 63 in 2016, and [entered] the top 50 at 38 in June 2018. We've been included in the Best of London awards since we opened, but because these are not things I've aimed for, there's no reason to take my foot off the pedal. You see all the time how a young chef has formulated his or her menu; they get their star, and then that's basically it. Often you find that the restaurant plateaus or declines. We have another five years to go before I hit my first big milestone.

How have you seen London's culinary scene evolve in the last five to 10 years? In the last two to three years? In 2005 to 2006, I was of the opinion that the London scene was dead or, at best, boring. I went to New York City because I felt there was value and quality at every price point. We didn't have good food available at low price points [in London]. I think there has since been a broadening of the quality of the offering in London at various price points, and an increase in ethnic foods available.

I've now been cooking in East London for 12 to 13 years. Thirteen years ago, we saw St. John Bread & Wine open. A wave of bars opened, but they were generally bad. Now, people eat out more often and spend a lot of disposable income eating in restaurants. What they spend per meal has increased. Even though you have an economic belt tightening, people spend more because there are better options at a lower price point, meaning they can still eat out a few times per week.

The Clove Club opened in Shoreditch in 2013 as part of a second wave of quality restaurants. There's now a new wave of restaurants that are similar to Lyle's operating at a similar price point with care put into the food. They're not fancy; rather, they're an evolution of a

Left: Chef James Lowe.

Whelk & Mayonnaise, Lyle's.

Whelk & Mayonnaise, Lyle's.

neighborhood wine bar and cafe concept.

Mid-market restaurants and chains are suffering with diners ordering food through UberEats and other delivery services, getting food delivered twice a week. We've suffered, too, because we're not a destination restaurant or a casual restaurant. We are slightly more expensive as a restaurant. You need to be of a certain income to eat here. How long can this go on? Last year was a tough one for this industry, but we're doing 25 percent over the previous year.

How would you describe the concept of Lyle's? We offer à la carte for lunch. We serve a set menu in the evenings, and [more recently], an à la carte bar menu as well. We want you to feel when you come in that you don't have to worry about the food. All you have to do is choose the wine. We serve good food by a well-informed team, at a reasonable price point. The menu is a reflection of the best ingredients available at any given time.

Why the name Lyle's? It was my grandmother's family name. She died two years before the restaurant opened. We sold her house and used the money to open the restaurant. I felt it was uniquely fitting. It was quite personal, which maybe the restaurant is as well.

Do you think customers in London are changing what they look for in a dining experience? I've grown very tired of when something is overused—it starts to lose meaning. I don't know that people know what nose-to-tail really means anymore. People use it in a restaurant that I wouldn't consider nose-to-tail at all. Farm-to-table doesn't mean anything. Even bad food comes from a farm. It's kind of the most ridiculous phrasing. We treat everything with a common sense philosophy—you do things that make sense to you, that have an ethical rationale behind them. When people use the term "zero waste," it doesn't make environmental or financial sense. We work with people who work responsibly and care about what they do. They don't waste food or damage the environment. They look after their livestock, farm, and pay attention to how they fish, taking responsibility in what they do because they care. You tend to find it all starts falling in line. Why wouldn't you work this way? Surely, this is the most obvious way of working.

Where do you look for inspiration currently? What keeps you fresh? It always comes from the producers. We speak to fishermen in the morning and they tell us what's available. I then look to find something else to complement the fish and we work the menu together in that way. There are some chefs who conceive a dish, draw something on paper of how they want it to look, and then they go and find out where to buy those ingredients. We work with several small farms that can't supply everything on their own that we need. I source a large amount of produce across a few farms, and we work out how to fit it into the menu puzzle.

We get produce picked from 3 a.m. to 4 a.m., then couriered straight to the restaurant. There will always be green peas or asparagus on the menu when they are available.

It seems the bar menu has taken off. Are you working on any other updates with the restaurant? We are always looking to refine the way we do things. We are a lot busier this year, so we are making sure we have the right team. We're tightening our processes and continuing to work to reduce wastage. I'm figuring out how to empower people on the team to help with the ordering and menu writing. Many on our staff have been here for at least two years, and we're looking at what can we do to educate, train, and bring them more into the operations. The restaurant itself will improve as a result.

What are some of your favorite restaurants in London right now when you have a day off? River Café. I wish I could afford to go all of the time. I go a few times a year, because it's amazing. It's now 35 years old! Also, I like Bright, in Hackney ; 40 Maltby Street; and Brawn.

Where do you like to visit when you travel outside of London? Food always influences wherever I travel, be

Broccolo, Three Cornered Garlic, & Cured Bonito, Lyle's.

it restaurants or something to see from a foreign culture. Last year, I visited Peru. It was a trip organized with Peruvian chef Diego Muñoz, an alumni of El Bulli and Mugaritz. We went up into the mountains. It was absolutely brilliant. Then we did a crazy crawl through Lima restaurants—starting at 7 a.m. and going through seven restaurants by the time we arrived at the airport at 6 p.m. You pack in as much as you can in a short period of time. I always like to see where the locals eat. It's not enjoyable to spend hours and hours in a restaurant. It's better to enjoy the time with the people you're with and move on to enjoy another thing. I also look for things we don't have in London, like grilled prawns.

I've been eating at Septime in Paris now for seven to eight years and I feel like Bertrand [Grébaut] is one of the best and most interesting chefs anywhere. There is still so much desire to drive the restaurant forward. He offers a great price point and the restaurant is always full. He could charge more now, but the team enjoys what they do and never go greedy, or overly ambitious. Grébaut understands the value of serving five to six simple dishes with a bit of creativity. That formula has worked and the food is phenomenal.

When it comes to ingredients, are there any benefits to being in London? Absolutely. Right now in London, there are a lot of good, small producers outside of the city. It's one thing that's helping us become more interesting than Paris at the moment. It's a very entrepreneurial time and a lot of people are embracing technology. We are a transportation hub. There's a startup whose sole job is to assist small producers in getting their products into London markets. Small producers are struggling with selling in regions where they produce, while places in London are willing to pay a high price for their products. We make sure that when we find a new, small producer that we're able to grow with them. We set up a courier system so we get the peas fresher than anyone else from this farm.

We also spend one to two days per week driving into the countryside to fruit farms to pick our own fruit and bring it back to London. Some ingredients we can only get if we go and source them ourselves. A lot of people buy ingredients from markets in Milan, Paris, and Spain; in London, we have access to a huge amount of produce, and the best ingredients in this country. It's always just 24 hours away. I don't think modern British food has to be British produce. No one grows the varieties of radicchio that are available in Italy. They are my favorite things in the world, so I buy loads of them when they are in season. We'll serve radicchio salads at lunch time, and with game at dinner. Tonight we're serving grilled Treviso with homemade mustard and homemade cider vinegar.

Do you have any new projects in the works for 2019? We're opening a new wine bar and bakery this year in Borough Market. And I'm also starting a book this year.

I had these ambitions around our fifth birthday, but we've been so busy that I have not had the time. I had a baby girl a year ago, which occupies all of my spare time. My aim is to build a team of people who want to be involved in the book as well. Our pastry chef has been with us for three years, and we have our sous chef, whom I'll be making head chef this year. It takes a lot of pressure off me. We will produce a collection of docu-style images and dish images for the book, and self-publish.

In the last three years, we have hosted over 15 guest chefs at the restaurant. I want diners to see what's happening elsewhere in the world. The guest chef series runs for one week, once per year. I invite five chefs from around the world, typically from countries where they don't have game or wild food culture, and fly them into Scotland, where I show them animals in their natural habitat. For three days, we do deer stalking, bird shoots, and fly fishing. When we do our game event, the goal is for the chefs to not do dishes from their restaurants. Instead, we force the chefs to create new dishes. We cook two dinners—one on Friday and one on Saturday. Each night we write and serve a different menu. The dishes are

Grilled Dried Mackerel & Preserved Gooseberry, Lyle's.

to pick our own fruit and bring it back to London. Some ingredients we can only get if we go and source them ourselves. A lot of people buy ingredients from markets in Milan, Paris, and Spain; in London, we have access to a huge amount of produce, and the best ingredients in this country. It's always just 24 hours away. I don't think modern British food has to be British produce. No one grows the varieties of radicchio that are available in Italy. They are my favorite things in the world, so I buy loads of them when they are in season. We'll serve radicchio salads at lunch time, and with game at dinner. Tonight we're serving grilled Treviso with homemade mustard and homemade cider vinegar.

Do you have any new projects in the works for 2019? We're opening a new wine bar and bakery this year in Borough Market. And I'm also starting a book this year.

I had these ambitions around our fifth birthday, but we've been so busy that I have not had the time. I had a baby girl a year ago, which occupies all of my spare time. My aim is to build a team of people who want to be involved in the book as well. Our pastry chef has been with us for three years, and we have our sous chef, whom I'll be making head chef this year. It takes a lot of pressure off me. We will produce a collection of docu-style images and dish images for the book, and self-publish.

In the last three years, we have hosted over 15 guest chefs at the restaurant. I want diners to see what's happening elsewhere in the world. The guest chef series runs for one week, once per year. I invite five chefs from around the world, typically from countries where they don't have game or wild food culture, and fly them into Scotland, where I show them animals in their natural habitat. For three days, we do deer stalking, bird shoots, and fly fishing. When we do our game event, the goal is for the chefs to not do dishes from their restaurants. Instead, we force the chefs to create new dishes. We cook two dinners—one on Friday and one on Saturday. Each night we write and serve a different menu. The dishes are never going to be repeated. One year, we did a tamale dish. No one had done that before in London. The guest chef doesn't even do that dish at his restaurant because he doesn't have the same ingredients available. I've never done an event like it anywhere else and I think diners want to attend it because there is nothing else like it. The game event is a series I'm really proud of. We try to make sure it's great for the guests, the kitchen, for me, and the visiting chefs.

Sometimes, the guest chef and I will write the menu together, but it's a bit arrogant to say that people want to see a menu from the mind of two chefs. It's a bit pretentious. Recently, we hosted Jowett Yu from Ho Lee Fook. There's nothing like his food in London. After attending the dinners, guests tend to see that there are some really amazing things happening outside of London. Patrons are very happy to see that there's a London bubble happening at the moment, but I've always judged Lyle's against what's happening in other cities around the world, not just in London.

Ultimately, people come to see a restaurant they're not going to get a chance to go visit.

If you had it to do over again, would you change anything? I was quite naive when we opened. I tried to do too much, too soon. I had a team of people in the kitchen who didn't get how I wanted to work. We changed the menu too often. The restaurant was too different from what I'd done before and so divergent from anything that had been done in London. On top of that, I made it too difficult for everyone. Now, I aim to understand the importance of being better organized.

What coffee are you serving in the restaurant right now? Initially, we wanted to serve coffees from places we'd heard of in Australia, the [United] States, and other parts of Europe. With a falling [British] pound, it made coffee [sourced internationally] more expensive to buy. As a result, more local roasters have opened in London, so, not intentionally, we've ended up supporting more local roasters. We identify who we think is doing something interesting in coffee, and in the process, you realize that there's seasonality in coffee, just as much as there is in food and wine. It's crazy that there still aren't many places that highlight that.

How do you handle challenges in running Lyle's? I feel like you have to stay very malleable. I try and establish a structure and make the team clear on what our principles are and the way we do what we do. I've found that if people stay with you and understand how you work, and why you do things a certain way, it makes you freer and more adaptable to change. If everything is overly prescribed, recipe-d, and set in stone, you're not able to handle changes and it gets incredibly boring. Being adaptable is also something that makes many restaurants successful. I try to approach it with an open mind. We just hope that people will always want to eat in a really good restaurant.

–

The Meals That Made Me

Words by Imogen Lepere
Photography by Daniela Velasco

Have you ever tried "Oxchoc," the beef-flavoured Twix bar based on a Victorian recipe? How about a glass of rabbit tea that's hot on one side and cold on the other? Both are on offer at The Fat Duck, Heston Blumenthal's three Michelin-starred restaurant in the tiny village of Bray. Part scientist, part magician-chef, Blumenthal has literally reconstructed the way diners all over the world experience food.

His inspiration is largely drawn from early childhood experiences. In fact, the entire menu at The Fat Duck, which opened in 1995, is structured around a single day at the seaside, with whimsical dishes such as "then we went rockpooling." Even the petit fours arrive in a dollhouse that's a replica of his childhood home.

Over the 24 years that The Fat Duck has been operating, Blumenthal has encouraged chefs to rethink long-held cooking techniques and challenge preconceptions about the interplay between savoury and sweet flavors and texture. More than anything, he has delved deeper into the link between flavour and memory to an unprecedented degree, leaving a lasting legacy for a new wave of young chefs.

Inspired by Heston Blumenthal's fascination with childhood, five London chefs shared an early memory that continues to influence their cooking today.

SELIN KIAZIM, OKLAVA AND KYSERI
Modern Cypriot small plates cooked with soul.

Before I opened my first restaurant, Oklava, I spent hours wondering how I could make my food unique. My thoughts kept returning to the long, hot summers I spent with my grandparents in a small village called Yeşilirma in northwestern Cyprus.

By the time my sisters and I woke up, my grandparents would usually be on their second break already. They were very early risers, tending to fields of citrus trees, strawberries, and Mediterranean vegetables. Dede [grandfather] was normally tucking into a large watermelon in the shade of a vine tree, while Nene [grandmother] would be toasting some of her home-baked bread over a wood-fired oven, before topping it with strawberry jam and a few slices of *hellim* [halloumi]. It was absolute heaven.

We'd spend the afternoons at my uncle's restaurant, a rustic shack right on the beach. The table was always groaning under skewers of sizzling lamb, pieces of chicken dressed in *kekik* [wild oregano] and lemon, fluffy pita breads, salad, and velvety hummus. Those lunches lasted for hours.

These memories are what created Oklava. Every morning we make Nene's bread and dress it with *kekik*, lemon juice, olive oil, and honey. Of course we also make the national dish of Cyprus, *şeftali kebab* ["sausage without skin" that uses caul fat to wrap the ingredients instead of sausage casing], just like at my uncle's restaurant.

I've realised that I can't reinvent cooking, nor do I need to. Instead, I aim to make delicious dishes that give people new food memories. Maybe I've finally worked out what my unique thing is: I try and cook with as much heart as my grandmother did and I think people can taste that.

KYSERI
KYSERI

Beef & Sour Cherry Manti and Kyseri Salad, Kyseri.

Erişte, Walnuts, Lemon Braised Greens, Sage, Egg Yolk & Tulum Cheese, Kyseri.

JEREMY CHAN, IKOYI
International, using the myriad spices found throughout West Africa.

My strongest food memory will always be enjoying dim sum with my family on Sundays when I was growing up in Hong Kong. We would eventually split up and scatter across the globe, our reunions far less frequent but no less meaningful.

The dish that evokes them particularly is Shanghainese freshwater prawns, which have a uniquely sweet flavour and are typically steamed with vinegar and ginger. I remember them as pearlescent balls, like corn kernels in size and shape, paired with mounds of fluffy rice. I've never since eaten prawns so sweet and perfect in texture.

I am still obsessed with taste and devouring beautiful things, and that dish continues to influence my cooking today. For example, texture is a critical component of a successful recipe, in my opinion, and there must also be a balance of sweet, salty, umami, and sour notes. Most importantly, it has influenced my cooking in the sense that I want my guests at Ikoyi to feel that same sense of happiness that I had as a child, demolishing the most perfect prawns in the world while surrounded by people who loved me.

We do serve a rice and prawn dish at Ikoyi. While it is not a replica of the original, the carefully balanced flavours and incredible burst of the prawns paired with al dente rice grains aims to capture that feeling of wonder. I can't get my hands on those special prawns over here unfortunately, so I cure mine in a slightly sweet syrup which gives them a similar bouncy quality.

One of my best recent memories was seeing Michelin three-starred Japanese chef, Mr. Araki, devouring a bowl of it and exclaiming "*Oishi!*," which means delicious. And, of course, I always make prawn rice for my family whenever we get together again.

MERLIN LABRON-JOHNSON, THE CONDUIT
French farm-to-table with a focus on traditional techniques.

I grew up in a poor household in South Devon, on the edge of a small market town called Buckfastleigh—home to Riverford Organics, pioneers of the vegetable box delivery programme. As a child, I was free to roam the countryside and would often find myself wandering into one of Riverford's fields. I became curious about the vegetables that grew there: kohlrabi, *swede* [rutabaga], purple potatoes, and exotic varieties of pumpkin.

Occasionally, I'd find them discarded by the edge of the tracks, as they had fallen off the back of a tractor. I would take them home to whizz into soups or bake, just to see what they'd taste like. Eventually, my parents signed up to receive a weekly box; it felt like Christmas every time.

Exploring the fields inadvertently turned me into an expert on the seasonality of British produce from a very young age. The concept of being creative with surprise combinations of locally harvested vegetables and treating them with the respect they deserve is the foundation of how I cook today.

In London, most of my produce comes from small, organic, and biodynamic farms in the West Country. I have an ongoing dialogue with my farmers whereby they update me on which vegetables are at their best and I build menus around this information.

Once a week, we receive a delivery box from my friends at the Husbandry School in Ashburton, whom I've known since I was eight years old. I try to commit to using everything they grow, partly to expand my creative horizons and partly because that's what I believe a sustainable relationship with a farm should be: a collaboration and a constant source of inspiration.

White Asparagus from Provence, Anchovies & Cedro Skin, Ikoyi.

Chef Jeremy Chan, Ikoyi.

TOM BROWN, CORNERSTONE
Seafood-focused, with a simplicity that lets the ingredients speak for themselves.

Ray wing was the first fish I ever remember eating, as it was a favourite of my dad's. Because of the wing's structure, the meat peels off the skeleton beautifully and just flakes away. It's so delicate and pleasing.

I grew up in Cornwall, and Dad and I would go fishing together fairly regularly. We'd throw back most of what we caught; it was more about spending time together than anything else, but we always took home the ray. Dad used to skin it, dust it in flour, and pan fry it in lashings of butter from the local farm. Looking back now, he made a right mess of the kitchen—almost every implement dirty and flour all over his clothes. But it was always delicious.

When I worked for Nathan Outlaw (of the Michelin two-starred restaurant Nathan Outlaw), we didn't serve much ray wing, but as soon as I opened my own restaurant, Cornerstone, it was the first thing on the menu. We currently serve it with a roast chicken butter sauce which is just beautiful. It's super-creamy and has layers of intense umami flavour. Dad always managed to get the frilly ends of the wing beautifully crisp and golden and that's exactly how I like to serve it now.

When we opened in April of 2018, Dad drove up from Cornwall for lunch and ordered the ray wing. It was a very proud moment, to cook his favourite fish for him the way he used to prepare it for me.

JAMES COCHRAN, 1251
Modern British ingredients with St. Vincentian and Scottish influences.

Food was the mainstay of the Cochran household. Our home in Whitstable, Kent, was constantly filled with the smell of fresh banana bread and sizzling spices—my mum was an amazing cook and the reason that I became a chef. She was from St. Vincent, a small Grenadine island with a food scene that draws inspiration from Africa, France, and the Caribbean. Her cooking always showed off this heritage with pride.

My favourite meal was Sunday lunch because we normally had a West Indian-influenced roast, an explosion of exotic flavours. Often, it would be jerk-spiced lamb leg with cauliflower cheese, crispy plantain, breadfruit, and a simple side of carrots.

From a chef's perspective, it looks like a confusion of influences, but it completely opened my mind to new flavours and how you can mix the unexpected. It paved the way to my current style of cooking—an eclectic combination of flavours that express my Caribbean, Scottish, and Kentish roots.

At my restaurant, 1251, we have buttermilk-jerk fried chicken served with Scotch bonnet jam, corn nuts, and coriander, which has become something of a signature. We also have a goat sharing dish: goat haunch rubbed in my own jerk spice seasoning and seared over hot coals. Desserts on the menu also nod to my St. Vincentian roots, with flavours that remind me of the sunshine, such as coconut parfait with white chocolate and mango.

I know that my future cooking will always be influenced by my past to some degree—by Mum's childhood in the Caribbean and the way she raised me to be proud of where I come from.

–

Darling

Words by Megan Krigbaum
Photography by Maureen M. Evans

Charlotte Wilde defines "darling" as such: "An affectionate and familiar term of address for a person or thing that is dearly loved or held in great favor. It's a positive, nice word."

It's also the name of her forthcoming restaurant, wine bar, and creative event space, a project that she's been building for the better part of a decade and plans to realize this year.

Wilde is a familiar face in the London wine scene; she's been crucial in helping usher in a new era of wine-drinking in the city. Like so many in the business, Wilde, a former ballerina, stumbled into working in restaurants in her twenties and never stopped. Having lived and worked in wine around the world (including harvests in California, Chile, and France), in 2012, she and her then-husband returned to London and launched a pop-up wine bar in Shoreditch, a brazen response to London's stodgier wine culture. "I just couldn't understand why it had to be this big kerfuffle," Wilde says. "I kept wondering, 'Why can't anyone just do really cool shit by the glass?'" And so they did, pouring cult bottles from Burgundian producers like Dujac, Roulot, and Leflaive by the glass in a convivial setting.

The immediate success of their pop-up made finding investors relatively easy and the two opened a bona fide wine bar, Sager + Wilde, in Hackney the next year. The corner bar became a beacon for the international avant garde wine set—it still is. And while Wilde is no longer involved in that business, it solidified her role in the city as a guru in all things wine.

It wasn't as if London didn't have a wine scene before Wilde got in the game. Despite its diminutive nature, England has always been a big player in the global wine market. And London, following suit, is arguably the wine capital of world. This is not hyperbole. Berry Bros. & Rudd, a wine shop on St. James's Street has been there for 320 years. There's 67 Pall Mall, a wine club where members can store away bottles to drink with friends and where the bar has a shocking 750 wines available by the glass, including

Noble Rot.

Slipsole & Smoked Butter, Noble Rot.

Pork, Pistachio & Prune Terrine and Senorio Ibérico Bellota Paleta D.O.P., Noble Rot.

Phil Bracey, Bright.

Grilled Leeks & Fresh Cheese, Bright.

Left: Ali Duncan. Right: Katsu Sando , Bright

old vintages of premier cru Bordeaux. London's patron wine saint Jancis Robinson is the best-known wine critic on the planet. And the city was way out in front of much of the world (save for Paris) when it came to natural wine-only bars, with pét-nat finding its way into renegade spots in the early 2000s.

Wilde sees the past six or seven years as the golden age of wine bars in London—and now wonders if maybe there might even be too many at this point. She's confident that just about anyone ("My 12-year-old niece," she says, offering an example of just about anyone) can come up with a wine list and pair wine with food, but she now has her eye on moving bar culture forward again.

In this interim before opening Darling, Wilde's been called on to advise on a wine delivery app (in London, you can have a bottle as fast as a pizza in New York City), as well as wine programs around town, and as a cellar consultant for people who want to collect and travel throughout the world of wine. She's currently working on a top secret "traveling hotel."

In conceiving and designing Darling, she's calling on her novel sensibility for aesthetics and playfulness. Whereas wine as a subject can often be a little uninviting, Wilde's mission is to give it texture and accessibility. In this, she's considering all of the trappings of a restaurant space—everything from the customers to the cost to the servers to the lighting to the scent of the soap in the bathroom. "All these things create an experience; it's so much more than just going, 'Here's a wine list.'"

Which is not to say that the wine for Darling will be an afterthought. Wilde's wine interests are wide-ranging, incorporating more conventionally made bottles alongside natural ones, with an emphasis on small producers. "Esoteric things are always really inspiring because it's what keeps things fresh," she says. "For example, there are unbelievable wines coming out of Tenerife, from Envinate, or England, like Ancre Hill in Wales, [as well as] Croatia, Lebanon, [and] Slovenia." Moving beyond the idea of offering more culty bottles by the glass, Wilde's goal is to open up more of the wine world to her guests.

All of this will find its way to Darling, a multifunctional space that Wilde says will be for everyone, a neighborhood place that people come back to all the time—for dates, for birthdays, for Sunday lunch with their kids. The food will not be overwrought and the vibe will take center stage.

For right now, Darling's location is a little up in the air, which means Wilde anticipates a summer opening, despite not having a site quite locked in. The Dalston space Wilde had been so smitten with, which was at one time a pie and mash shop and another time a local Chinese restaurant, has proven more difficult than expected. But she is crystal clear about the fact that Darling belongs in Dalston neighborhood. And it's clear why: "You've got Ridley Road Market that's got everything from Nigerian fabric print shops to Bangladeshi kitchens to fishmongers, Spanish food stores, and a really gorgeous Italian wine shop. And then there's a shopping center with discount stores and everything. And then there's Kingsland High Street station. Kingsland High Street runs from Tottenham all the way down to Liverpool Street. And then round the back, you've got De Beauvoir, with multimillion-pound houses. It's right in the middle of everything," she says.

There, nestled in this vibrant commotion, the sounds, the smells, the locals, will be Darling, London's wine way forward.

–

SIDEBAR: Charlotte Wilde's Guide to Drinking Wine in London Now

Brat

Chef Tomos Parry has garnered heaps of attention for his nuanced, wood-fired cooking at year-old Brat. The restaurant's wine list is just as subtly precise, broken into "Easy Drinkers," "The Classics," and "Off the Beaten Track" selections.
bratrestaurant.com

Noble Rot

"They've got the best list in London," says Wilde. The selection from owners Mark Andrews and Dan Kealing takes into account the Old World classics, conventional wines and bottles from smaller producers. "The best producers in the world are there," she says. "And they have a really great tone of voice; they are not an amalgamation of lots of other people's ideas and styles, which does happen from time to time."
noblerot.co.uk

The Draper's Arms

"My favourite pub in London," says Wilde. "The wine list has such a vast range and is lovingly and organically put together by owner and publican Nick Gibson. You can lose hours, if not days of your life in that beautiful pub and wine list."
thedrapersarms.com

Bright

This small London Fields wine bar and restaurant is the newest from the owners of popular P. Franco and wine shop Noble Fine Liquor, with a natural wine-leaning list and vegetable/seafood-leaning menu.
brightrestaurant.co.uk

Leroy

Shoreditch's Leroy was opened by two sommeliers, Ed Thaw and Jack Lewens, along with chef Sam Kamienko, all formerly of restaurant Ellory. The wine list is concise, but loaded with bottlings from the most forward-thinking producers in Europe.
leroyshoreditch.com

Wine Car Boot

For the past couple years, Wilde's good friend Ruth Spivey has been hosting what Wilde describes as "get-togethers and celebrations of all the elements that make wine so enjoyable." Spivey has created mobile wine markets, working with independent wine stores who create pop-up shops, selling bottles and pouring glasses from the trunks of cars (wine boots).
winecarboot.com

Pork, Pistachio & Prune Terrine and Señorío Ibérico Bellota Paleta D.O.P., Noble Rot.

Open Fire

Words by Jacqueline Larkin
Photography by Maureen M. Evans

Brat, a Michelin-starred restaurant located in London's fashionable Shoreditch district, is the first solo venture of Welsh-raised chef Tomos Parry. Parry's barbecuing prowess was first cultivated during a notable post at Kitty Fisher's in Mayfair.

Parry's culinary skill with an open fire, paired with a dedication to a farm-to-table ethos, is a modern homage to an age-old method to cooking, when a source of heat and simple, quality ingredients were the essential elements of a dish. Inspired by the boisterous, social atmosphere of the pintxo bars of San Sebastian, Spain, the restaurant is named after the colloquial Old English term for turbot ("bratt"), which also happens to be its signature dish. Weaving these influences together, Brat capitalizes on the ubiquitous open-fire cooking trend that has swept the nation. Yet amidst the clamor of chefs hoping to leave their mark with an exposed flame, Parry distinguishes himself from the rest.

Adhering to a mantra of "Just serve it simply," Parry's no-nonsense approach to cooking reveals the ingredients of a dish rather than obscuring them beneath unnecessary accoutrements of drizzled syrups and flavored foams. His focus is on serving unpretentious food in a tasteful manner. "For me," says Parry, "the simple pleasure of eating well is what Brat is all about. It's a place I would want to eat—whether that be one dish with a glass of wine at lunch or settling in at the bar for a few hours." This guiding methodology is apparent in plates like the chopped egg salad with bottarga: a warm and welcoming dish composed of a thick slice of toasted sourdough bread, topped with a rich, languid yolk, crushed boiled egg, light greens, and savoury shavings of cured mullet roe. The dish, much like the restaurant itself, is a bold study in simplicity that is precise, purposeful, and delicious.

The seasonal rotation of dishes is a deliberate orchestration of the restaurant's commitment toward ethical sourcing and low-intervention farming. This sentiment is best captured by the grilled turbot dish that gives the restaurant its name.

Right: Chef Tomos Parry.

RUMANS • BURTO
ED

Burnt Cheescake & Rhubarb, Brat.

BRAT
BRAT
A RESTAURANT & WINE BAR
BRAT
LANGOUSTINE
YOUNG LEEKS
WHOLE TURBOT
BEEF CHOP
+
100 WINES

Smoked Cod's Roe, Brat.

Turbot, Brat.

Turbot is a type of fish that is typically pan-fried, steamed, or poached due to its delicate and mildly flavored flesh. Parry, instead, places a whole turbot in a metal cage and grills it over lumpwood charcoal. "The key to cooking this dish is to develop and celebrate the unique texture of the turbot. The dish relies on quality fish with distinct terroir cooked with gentle-burning charcoal with minimum intervention," describes Parry. "The grilling methods that inspired us were developed and refined in the fishing town of Getaria, techniques mastered by explorers cooking on their ships, which gradually made their way onto land and into the kitchens of the fishermen and local restaurants." A subtle mix of oil, vinegar, and gelatine from the turbot produces a "pil-pil"-style sauce, which is basted over the fish as it gently cooks. The turbot emerges from this slow-grill method with a golden char of its rich, oily skin, before it is bathed in an emulsion of its own juices to bring out the natural fattiness and flavour of its pearly, white flesh.

Brat's dining room is equal parts rugged and regal. A set of narrow stairs leads up into a warm, open space infused with light, set above the ground-floor Smoking Goat restaurant. There's an intimate arrangement of tightly packed tables, wood-clad walls, and a roaring open kitchen filled with wood-fired grills, which emit a tantalizing chicory aroma. The posh, yet relaxed aesthetic allows patrons to focus on the simple pleasure of eating. But the space has character. Even the original wood flooring is a holdover from the venue's past as a pole-dancing pub.

A wall is lined by a varied wine collection. For ease of selection, the collection is cleverly categorized as crowd favourites, classics, and maverick blends, rather than by region or style. Each month, the restaurant features a particular producer's flagship wine, usually a low-intervention, natural blend, which it sells by the glass or bottle. A recent favourite hails from Greece, a country which has one of the oldest, and historically, most tumultuous, wine-making traditions in the world. Xinomavro, one of Greece's finest red grapes still remains fairly unknown on the international stage due to its fickle cultivation. The wine is described as "reminiscent of a young nebbiolo with a distinctly Greek accent. Bursting with blackberry and damson with savoury notes of dried herbs, tomato, and olives." Winemaker Apostolos Thymiopoulos, one of Brat's featured producers, is representative of a new generation and of the kind of producers the restaurant seeks to work with, bringing Xinomavro to the rest of the world in a "modern, high-quality form."

Overall, Brat boldly embodies the open-fire cooking of Basque country, where smoked potatoes crisped in golden butter, and where lightly blanched greens, pristine fillets of fish, savoury portions of duck and rabbit, and sizzling chops of beef and lamb are prepared with skilled restraint. Parry's back-to-basics approach may, at face value seem deceptively simple. Yet, therein lies the subtle complexity of the master chef's culinary trick: he makes the precise and sophisticated appear effortless in execution.

–

Pie Franco

Words by James Hansen
Photography by Maureen M. Evans

"What's essentially a glorified wine shop isn't everyone's idea of a great night."

That glorified wine shop, amongst a scraggle of corner shops, chicken restaurants, and East Enders on the thrum of Lower Clapton Road, is P. Franco. And the man who told me that is Phil Bracey, an apparently unserious, slightly ragamuffin Aussie with a penchant for caps, who could talk for hours about the specifics of low intervention winemaking in Alsace, France, but won't, because he thinks that's fucking boring. He's also general manager of P. Franco, which has quietly and quickly become one of London's most interesting places to eat—without ever being a restaurant. It's an awful lot of people's idea of a great night.

It began as a local adjunct. Owners Liam Kelleher and James Noble already had Noble Fine Liquor, a natural/biodynamic wine retail shop on Broadway Market, one of East London's most gastronomic rambles. The early days on Lower Clapton Road were basic, but the service and quality were no less generous than they are now: servers pour glasses according to taste, rather than from a prescriptive list, and supplement the wine with impeccably sourced cheese and charcuterie. Maverick winemakers like Pierre Frick—an Alsatian legend known for ripping out neighbors' vines he deemed impure—found both church and congregation here.

London's wine gurus came like moths to a flame. Even the name, chosen for its echo of *pie franco*—the Latin phrase referring to ungrafted heritage, noble rootstocks—inspired reverence. Tegan Ella Hendel's typographic art decorates the place with authority and wit. The room is flanked by shelf upon shelf of bottles with distractingly oversized graphics and illustrations. But the energy concentrates on the massive concrete counter, in a space no more than ten paces per side. The space has *it*.

Bracey, though, saw a problem. "When I started at P. Franco, I was told by many people both from within the industry and outside of it how much they loved it. However that same love didn't seem to translate into bums on seats. There seemed to always be this complete lull during the evening right at dinner time as the food offering at the time was simply cheese and charcuterie." Such lulls are a much bigger concern for restaurants than they are for wine shops, but nonetheless, the lull was solved—even if it didn't really need solving—by one chef and two induction hobs.

William Gleave was, and still is, an Australian chef who had worked at Garagistes, a restaurant in Tasmania. That restaurant is now closed, but its sensibility—a descendent of Ben Shewry's Attica, a prelude to Dan Hunter's Brae—influences Gleave, weaving with what he learned in his time at two London landmarks. He spent time at 40 Maltby Street, a darling of the industry and perhaps the perfect definition of a hidden gem located in a brick railway arch by the Thames. The other, Brawn, is a neighborhood restaurant in East London that looks like a wilder version of St. John, with shocks of bright artworks on its white walls.

Per Bracey, the food that started coming out of P. Franco "very much reminded me of a couple of places in Paris that were serving food that essentially had no place in being there—as in [the food] was way better than anticipated considering the space." The self-deprecating community that Kelleher and Noble had built—neatly summarised by Bracey as "it's just fermented grape juice, it's not really changing the world"—now had a chef on two induction hobs turning out food befitting the city's most lauded restaurants.

One of Hendel's earliest designs spoke to that self-deprecation: "P. Franco is now serving real food." In 2019, P. Franco began bringing in guest chefs from all over the world. Gleave was followed by Tim Spedding from London's The Clove Club; Spedding was followed by Giuseppe Lacorazza from Wildair's brigade in New York City; Lacorazza was followed by Giuseppe Belvedere from East London's Brawn; and Belvedere was followed by George Tomlin, who worked under Spedding at The Clove Club and shares Gleave's Australian background

Les Milans
Rotten
Les Aussigouins
HANAMI
AMATÉUS BOBI
RUBEN
FILIPPI
La Roche Bézigon
L'AUNIS ÉTOILÉ
LA LUNOTTE
LA LUNOTTE
Sancerre
Sancerre
Noble Rot
Wine From Another Galaxy
Eat London
SAUTERNES
Vin de France
Château Cambon
Château Cambon
le petit domaine
le petit domaine
CATHERINE BERNARD
CATHERINE BERNARD
ALESSANDRINO
VINI RABASCO VINO ROSSO CANCELLI

TUTTO
PETER
COOKSLEY
GEORGE
TOMLIN
14 09 18
14 09 18
14 09 18
P.FRANCO
MORTA
DELLA
PARTY

2016
Hermitage
RUBEN
109

from The Town Mouse in Melbourne. Anna Tobias followed, with a background at two of the city's most storied restaurants—The River Café and Rochelle Canteen—current chef Túbo Logier combines Spedding and Tomlin's Clove Club education with time at In De Wulf, much-missed by restaurant followers in its native Belgium and around the globe.

This is a succession of residencies, and so P. Franco's culinary history is not so much a lineage as an orbit: disparate chefs united by a culinary gravity, a style that bears no direct reference to country or cuisine. The food is not so much cooked or prepared as assembled. Cheese, charcuterie, and pasta feature regularly in whatever style the guest chefs choose. If dishes bear a hallmark, it is deceiving insouciance: fustiness is abhorred, tweezering is maligned, and each chef has free reign. Play and surprise are valued above all else.

Tim Spedding turned his palate towards Japan, with broths of seaweed and raw mackerel, except the mackerel is from the Cornish coast, and towards Italy, with agnolotti pasta in a broth of chicken and lemon thyme, except the pasta stuffed with English cheese. Gleave turned back towards Australia and its proximity to the Pacific coasts of Asia with squid noodles in XO sauce. Tobias aimed for the "modern British" cuisine that has come to represent a kind of London pride, but is also definitely kind of French and kind of Italian, serving bacon and white beans; sausage and green sauce instead of salsa verde; and a whole, burnished poached pear bobbing in a pool of finger-swiping custard. There's no spectral history weighing down the place with tradition.

The unifying theme, if there is one, is community. Lacorazza remembers his stint at P. Franco, saying, "Food was always better when it was crowded and people were having fun." Bracey remembers, "To sit and eat in the space that is P. Franco comes with it many concessions and creates many expectations. To fight against it instead of leaning into it or harnessing it wouldn't create the same harmonious convivial experience." And Dan Wilson, who was at P. Franco in the earliest days remembers the place having a distinctive energy, with a "kind approach and lackadaisical attitude to service."

It's a particular community, too. All of the chefs passing through name-check East London: the bleed out from Shoreditch into London Fields, Hackney Downs, and Clapton that has quietly usurped Soho as the nexus of contemporary dining in London. For Bracey, East London rarely feels like a city at all: "I tend to live a more suburban- and community-focused life and have generally stayed out of Central London." It is the neighborhood that might never have expected to have a trend-defining wine bar like P. Franco call it home.

What the laid-back "glorified wine shop" hides is that crucial restaurant truism: to break the rules, you have to understand them first. On a busy night, a truly busy night with plates set down on spare retail shelving, chef Anna Tobias runs a salad to the pass as octopus sautés, briefly unattended, in a pan. Happy chatter skits off the concrete counter. P. Franco's *bonhomie* is so infectious as to feel like a good mate's kitchen, where delays are part of the fun and mistakes cost ego rather than money.

Zooming out a little is to see how that confidence is marshalled by preparation. Pouring a wine to taste means knowing the wines inside out. Running while cooking requires timing down to the second. Keeping service swift and subtle among 30 people in a small space is a matter of system and structure as much as exchanging *bons mots* about last night's football. For Bracey, "There has to be an all-for-one mentality as corny as that may sound…where the duties are assigned to whoever feels they have the most amount of time to do it, it materialises in chefs mopping up after a busted pipe. It materialises everyday in a million and one different ways and that relationship both makes P. Franco and is what would prevent carbon copies of it."

P. Franco, located amidst a scraggle of corner shops and chicken restaurants, is a wine shop with stools, a table, two hobs, and a couple of wine experts who could be your flatmates who you never knew were wine experts. It has a short menu on paper that won't be the same as yesterday's or tomorrow's. Your flatmate-wine expert will ask you what you like—not what wine, vintage, or producer, just what—and pour you something that matches it. You'll eat from that menu. It will taste good. Behind it all will be the story of a restaurant scene unshackling itself from the expectations that once gave it the significance it craved. You'll eavesdrop stories of building rents peaking and troughing on surrounding streets, and trips to Parisian *caves à vin*, Italian *trattorie*, and Australian cafes. They all feel present here. But you're still finishing a glass of wine and a plate of food, touched by all those influences, at once on Lower Clapton Road, in East London.
–

Chef Anna Tobias, P. Franco.

Behind the Scenes: Supper Clubs

Words by John Moore
Photography by Adam Goldberg and Daniela Velasco

Staring at a locked, steel gate looking into what appears to be an industrial complex, we both asked, “How do we get inside?” My friend Jo and I had just arrived at Regent Studios, a tall, gray building from the 1970s, and home of that evening’s supper club. It had been a fun walk to get here, as we rambled quietly through London fields, weaved through the evening crowds filling the restaurants on Broadway Market, then turned along Regents Canal into an area that, within a few steps, transitioned into a deserted block. The only life on the street was the two of us staring at the gate.

Half of the fun of supper clubs is finding them. The feeling of adventure and mystery when finding a new place, tucked behind the main thoroughfares, enhances the evening’s ambiance. This evening was bound to have a strong start.

Just up the road, we spotted a taxi pulling up. I caught up with the group that emerged and asked, “By chance, are you going to the Vietnamese supper club?” They were. Our collective brainpower found the combination pad to unlock the gate. We were soon riding a rickety elevator with a loud hum that slowly took us to the third floor. I jumped when its doors slammed open onto an open-air hallway that neatly framed a beautiful red-orange sunset. After several steps, a warm smile stretched across my face as I saw strings of cafe lights reaching across the room ahead, gently illuminating the space we would soon enter.

The term “supper club” is hard to pin down. For me, it is a cross between a lively dinner party and eating at a newly opened restaurant. I am always surprised at how the atmosphere and diners differ. Some are outrageous, over-the-top affairs while others provide a warmer, cozier evening, often within the host’s home. At its core, a supper club is an evening of good food and good company, an opportunity to sit with and get to know new people. While it would be awkward to start a conversation with a nearby table in a restaurant, it is natural to talk with your neighbors at a supper club. If you are open to novelty and surprise, as I am, it’s fantastic.

I still vividly remember the first supper club I attended, on a clear evening in early June 2013. I arranged it as a surprise for my partner, yet I was more surprised—it easily surpassed my expectations and is one we still talk about today.

We went to James Ramsden’s new location for his Secret Larder supper club, a little wine shop and bar called Printers and Stationers. It was a very charming venue, nestled in a cobbled cove just off Columbia Road in East London. It was dimly lit with evening sun peeking in from the back garden and candles on paint-splattered wooden tables with mismatched chairs. On paper, it seemed similar to other bars and cafes in the neighborhood, but that night, it was the the only place where I wanted to be.

Six years later, and I can still hear the laughter mixed with conversations about social media, as a woman at our table was just hired as the social media director at Harrod’s. The upcoming couture shows she would attend in Paris were worlds away from my finance job. Ramsden has since opened several restaurants in London, like Pidgin, which is just up the road in Hackney. It’s a favorite stop for Sunday lunch and often has the feel of his earlier supper club. To this day, when I come across a bottle of Marcillac, I am immediately transported back to that evening when it was flowing freely on our table.

Memorable nights at supper clubs are still possible in London, and over time, I have grown more curious to learn what happens behind the scenes. Here’s what I learned about some recent favorites.

//

UYEN LUU
Vietnamese Supper Club in East London

It was Uyen’s supper club that was on the other side of that steel gate at Regent Studios. As a fan of Vietnamese food, I have been to Uyen’s several times for her traditional feast, which is even more delicious than many I have eaten in Vietnam. Her space is inviting—nothing matches but everything blends perfectly together. Upbeat music playing in the background accompanies the chopping of food in the kitchen area. Plants perched around the room intermingle with lamps emitting a soft glow. As the guests arrive, Uyen casually shows them to their seats while the air fills with the sound of guests introducing themselves.

As for the menu, the dishes can include rice noodles with crispy pork belly and julienned carrots, which provide a bright pop of color; shrimp dumplings with red peppers, which give them a hint of heat; chicken and papaya salad topped with fresh coriander has a bright, peppery tone; pork and mushroom rolls have just the right amount of tartness; and the most satisfying soup made with beef, pork, lemongrass, and noodles leaves me longing for more.

The crockery is a mixture of old and new. My favorites are the natural-colored earthenware plates made by Kana London, a potter who also had her workshop in Regent Studios (and introduced Uyen to the space) before

Imad's Syrian Kitchen.

Left: Labneh and Yallanji. Right: Chef Imad Alarnab, Imad's Syrian Kitchen.

moving to a building several blocks north. Uyen's food seems content in Kana's bowls. I recently met Uyen for a friendly visit and a cup of tea. She was moving between her refrigerator, oven, and counter as she prepped for a 50-person dinner party. I felt privileged to have a front-row seat, chatting with her while she was preparing the food.

What is that roasting in the oven? The aroma is so rich and savoury. It is just some fennel I am roasting… along with some secret spices.

Your supper clubs are always so perfectly timed with the food served at the right temperature and time. What is your secret? The cuisine lends really well to what I am doing. Most of the food can be kept at room temperature. It is small and Vietnamese food is all about the flavor within the small things. It is about eating plenty but in small portions. It lends well to a small kitchen because you can prep. You can make everything and then you pour hot broth over it. And it is that way because Vietnamese people depend on their street food livelihood. The food is created so that it can be prepped in advance, and then easily served with some hot broth.

Your supper clubs are often very playful. Is that something you're thinking about when you're prepping for a meal like this? It is very Vietnamese to eat playfully, and food is at the heart of it. There is even the expression "ăn chơi," that translates literally as "eat playfully," because Vietnamese eat all the time. You cannot just sit there and not eat anything. In Vietnam, instead of asking someone how they are, you greet them with "have you eaten yet?" It is always about eating and the food is so happy—so colorful, vibrant, and explosive—that it becomes playful at the heart of it.

What about London makes supper clubs so appealing? British people are known for being reserved and yet attending supper clubs is something they really like doing. I think what makes it work is the environment. If you say it is a supper club, people are willing to talk and share with each other. They like the idea of joining dinner parties and meeting other people. I think that is the main heartbeat of it—that you can meet other people.

Do you find that people actually communicate with one another?
Yes! I love that about my supper clubs. What I noticed early on is that people's sense of positivity can really affect the entire table and how people eat as well. If the food can be shared from a dish, it is like an icebreaker that they enjoy, and then they will start interacting with each other. Now I can tell when they are starting to interact, which makes for a fun night.

What were some inspirations that led you to starting your supper club? I really liked the idea of having people over for dinner. Every week, I would make food for friends and friends of friends and had a great time doing it.

I also spent a lot of time in Italy where they have osterias—a little restaurant downstairs in someone's farm or mountain home. Osterias are not advertised so you have to ask about them, which makes them feel more discovered. When I went to Tuscany last year, we were shopping inside a farm when they mentioned they offer dinners with their produce. I immediately shouted, "Oh, great!" And it was excellent. They brought out everything—there were 12 antipasti along with whatever pasta you wanted. It also had the most amazing views over Tuscany. It was just beautiful. I was really inspired by that.

Let's go back in time to 2009 when you first started. What do you remember about the first supper club you held in your home? The first time I had it, it was friends and bloggers who attended, and it was messy! It went on until 1 a.m., because I wasn't as oiled as I am now. And I was serving so much food so it took forever. But it was fun.

What was your most memorable supper club? After one supper club, everyone slept over. We were all sleeping in our chairs and on the floor. Some of the people I knew and some I had just met. Before I had major responsibilities, I was really open to so much fun. Then we all had breakfast the next morning. I can't remember who but someone started cooking and, soon after, we had a full breakfast in front of us and started eating again.

I have had such an amazing time doing this. One of the best times was also when some friends who are in Michael Buble's band came over. There were about five or six who came, and they brought their instruments, so there was loads of music and singing. I had a piano, and they brought their guitars and bass, and someone made something—I can't remember what—into a drum. It was such a great night.

What I find most genuine about your supper club is how you have integrated your mother into the process. Can you tell me more about that? She is traveling in Vietnam now, and I miss her, but when she is away, I push myself to experiment. It is more traditional when she is here, and I really appreciate having her help. My daughter also helps. She is three-and-a-half years old and she loves coming here. From a very young age, she was sitting here pulling herbs. Whatever she can do, she loves helping. Even if it is just putting stuff in a jar or other simple things, she just loves it.

My friends also help. Mostly they are my friends from years ago, and a few are food stylists from my food photography business. We get to spend time together every weekend, so it is a really joyous thing to be able to work with my friends and my family as well. They treat my space and my supper club as if it is their home. We love cooking and working together. It makes it a really nice time, to work hard but to also be with your friends and family and have proper chats when we are cooking. It is like a family kitchen.

Ten years running a supper club is a real success. How do you keep expanding the guest list? It is all by word of mouth. On Monday and Tuesday especially, I get many emails saying, "My friend has just been this weekend and she really liked it. I want to come." Recently one of my

Imad's
SYRIAN KITCHEN
CHOOSE
LOVE

BIRCHALL
55
57

Left: Falafel, Olive Salad, Shalal Salad, and Flatbread. Right: Syrian Ice Cream, Imad's Syrian Kitchen.

guests shared an Uber Pool to go home, and I soon received a call from someone saying, "I met someone in an Uber who told me about your supper club." It is really nice that someone is actually talking about me. I feel really lucky. It feels like the hard work pays off when it makes people happy and they recommend it.

Which came first, cooking or photography? I've always been a photographer but have only been doing it professionally for a few years. The supper club led me to food photography and food styling. I was a filmmaker before and then I owned several fashion boutiques in the West End.

As a hobby, I started the supper club and blogging, and people just kept coming. I had quite a mixed history before I landed here.

I have toyed with the idea of opening a restaurant, but I love my photography. I really like cooking for others, but I do not want to do that over my photography. I have struck the right balance where I get to cook once or twice a week and also work on my photography.

What are your favorite London destinations where you can escape and unwind? I absolutely love my fruit & veg shop—Clock Tower Fruit & Vegetables. There are a few scattered around. They have everything that you can imagine that is in season from all over the world, as well as all the good British food. My favorite thing to do for the supper club and general life is to shop in there. I just find it so fascinating that they have all the varieties of aubergines, all the varieties of tomatoes, and it nice to go and try new things. It inspires me to cook. And my daughter knows nearly every fruit and vegetable because we spend loads of time in there. She likes to help me there. If I ask her, "Can you find me a green tomato?" then in just a few moments, she is bringing me green tomatoes.

I also like Ally Pally Farmer's Market. It is a great way to spend a Sunday and the produce is delicious and beautiful.

For restaurants, The Delaunay on Aldwych, in Covent Garden, is a favorite escape. Anything on the menu is amazing, and their Sunday roast is the best. Even its mashed potatoes—they use some particular potato—are gorgeous. It is consistent. Its chicken curry is good; its Hungarian goulash is nice. Everything is well-prepared.

The sushi bar at Atari-Ya in Golders Green is another favorite spot. They supply most of the Japanese restaurants with fish. The sushi bar is a standard supermarket sushi bar, but it is really good. I highly recommend it.

//

IMAD'S SYRIAN KITCHEN: CHOOSE LOVE
Various venues with different menus.

"Choose Love." The name hung above a door just down the street from me on Columbia Road for several months before I could eat there. There were only 24 seats and they were always fully booked. One evening, I stopped by on a whim and there happened to be one open seat. With fate on my side, I grabbed it.

Inside was a calm, rustic neutral-colored space that Imad Alarnad said was similar in feel and layout to his house. He described how you pass through the kitchen to long dining tables filled with homemade Syrian food, just like in this space. The blue-and-white patterned bowls perfectly framed his dishes, which were allowed to shine against the room's neutral colors.

I had several chances to talk with Imad during my earlier attempts to eat there. He would take a break and join me outside on the sidewalk for casual conversation. I soon learned that three years earlier, he arrived in London, fleeing the Syrian civil war and the associated tragedy and loss. His trip to London was long and treacherous, as he passed through Lebanon, Turkey, Greece, Macedonia, Serbia, and then Hungary.

Imad shared that he owned several restaurants in Damascus before the war but they had since been destroyed. It was tough to digest yet he was optimistic about the cooking platform he was developing in London. He had several jobs outside the food industry when he arrived before rekindling his passion as a chef. He was now partnering with the charity "Help Refugees" to raise money for Hope Hospital, a children's hospital in Syria's Aleppo region.

Imad treats his guests at the Choose Love supper clubs and pop-up shops to sublime Syrian meals. The cuisine, as he describes it, is "traditional homemade Syrian food overflowing with spices and herbs learned from [his] mother. The aroma from mint and cumin remind me of Damascus." He prepares the dishes to be shared family-style, as they were in his family home.

I was filled with anticipation. He took us on a food journey that began with nine starters, including cheese and spinach pastries, hummus, *baba ghanoush* (a smoky, mashed eggplant puree), *bado* (young eggplants, sweet red peppers, and smoked chiles), *labneh* (a thick, sour yogurt) with watermelon, beet dip, olive salad, *shalal* (cheese) salad, *yallanji* (stuffed grape leaves), and a mound of flat bread. Following that, there were three main courses that included *kebab* (lamb), smoked chicken with rice, and *bamya* (a Syrian stew). I somehow found room for his evening's final course, a generous serving of Syrian ice cream. Outside of his supper clubs, his pop-up shops sell falafels that garner rave reviews.

This supper club was different from others that I had attended. As full and as happy as I felt from such a delicious dinner, I left with even more: Imad's positive and contagious energy resonated strongly with me. Here was someone who had faced challenges I could barely imagine.However rather than dwell on the past and the choices he could have made, he chose to look forward and find his way to help those less fortunate than he. And as exciting as the dinner was—tasting new food, meeting new people—experiencing Imad living his choice of love was what I found most fulfilling. I reflect on that often as his generosity and kind spirit reminded me that whenever and however I can, I should Choose Love.

–

EPITOME

132 COLUMBIA POTTERY
020 7729 2629
Imad's
CHOOSE LOVE
POLICE
BREAD COFFEE GOODS

Justifying Roots

Words by Georgie Carroll
Illustration by Lucia Ammadeo

We do not offer take-away service. The sign sits before the immaculate maître d' who silently, smiling, searches for my reservation. Her lacquered hair catches the amber lustre of whisky bottles in a display case. To my right, a staircase descends to a lower-level dining room, enclosed by the *jali* latticework typical of Mughal architecture. Once inside, the restaurant is like a train's dining car, subtle at first and then obvious. The embossed, jade velvet benches are a cue to carriage seats. But I only notice this as I bite into the amuse bouche: a miniature blue cheese *naan* washed down with a pumpkin and coconut *shorba* (soup). Looking around, there are other Indian accents: mythical birds in brass, monochrome photos of palace arches. The first course is Kashmiri morels with walnut powder and a Parmesan *pappadum*. Piano jazz plays as I stick a fork into the *burrata*, the tamarind of a classic *papdi chaat* mixing with tomato. There's pork on the menu too, which is a surprise. Pork is eaten widely in India but is a minority food almost impossible to find on menus. Other things surprise: wasabi in the *raita*, a *barfi*-meets-treacle-tart. I ask the waiter what makes the black dairy *daal* so delicious; I've never tasted one so buttery. "That's just regular, home-cooked *daal*," he says.

Indian Accent opened at the end of 2018, following the success of Manish Mehrotra's now chain restaurant brand in Delhi and New York. The food is global and regional. It reimagines the traditional and reworks the bounds of "Indian cuisine." Despite this, there's an inescapable element of nostalgia about the room. Almost all of London's iconic Indian restaurants speak, to different degrees, of a bygone time, whether it's the advent of the railway (Bombay Bustle), the Irani cafe (Dishoom), the colonial social club (Gymkhana), the influence of Bombay Art Deco (Dishoom Kensington), Victoriana (Lokhandwala), or even the early British curry house (Veeraswamy).

Since 2013, Gymkhana, only a short stroll from Indian Accent, has celebrated clubs where members of high society would socialise, drink, and play sports. Floral Victorian china mingles with mounted game heads. At the bar, reinterpreted colonial cocktails are garnished with curry leaves. (The classic "Quinine Sour" really shouldn't be missed—you start to wonder why you don't put ginger in *all* of your cocktails. There's a current bar menu inspired by pioneering women of India too. "Bombay Talkies" is an homage to Devika Rani, first lady of Indian cinema, a balance of elderberry and hibiscus liquors with a golden sugar cube and Champagne.) Gymkhana's "Hunter's Menu" offers quail, guinea fowl, and *muntjac* to share, with street food additions like *papads* and *bhel*. The tandoor roasted lamb loin with quail *tawa pulao* and quail eggs really is top drawer.

Indian food in Britain has always been something of a composite, a product of traditional recipes suited to Western tastes. The British created the concept of curry in the 18th century, reducing the various spiced dishes they had eaten on the subcontinent to a word that sounded like the Tamil *kaṟi*, meaning a spicy gravy made from vegetables or meat. Curry and rice has been served in London since the 1770s, by which time Indian ingredients and recipes such as spices and chutneys had already begun to influence Anglo cuisine. Evocative of British India, the dish became the house speciality of popular eateries in Piccadilly. The first Indian restaurant owned by an Indian opened in 1810, the Hindoostane Coffee House on George Street, Marylebone, the venture of surgeon and traveller Sake Dean Mahomed. The site of the restaurant can still be visited today, though it manifests only as a green plaque, marking it significant to the diverse cultural heritage of Westminster and to the renowned figures "who have made lasting contributions to society."

London's oldest extant Indian restaurant is Veeraswamy, established in 1926 by the great-grandson of an English general and a Mughal princess. Veeraswamy has hosted Gandhi, Nehru, and Churchill, as well as Chaplin and Brando. Its opulent interiors of cusped arches and palms evoked a maharaja's palace. Many early Indian restaurants took the lead from Veeraswamy, creating a romantic Indian aesthetic. The cliché is red-and-gold flocked wallpaper as backdrop to waiters dressed in uniform. In 1997, the restaurant became part of the group that includes Chutney Mary and Amaya. It gained its Michelin star in 2016. Today, Venetian-style chandeliers hang from silver-clad ceilings, and aureate walls are dressed with *kalighat* paintings from West Bengal, depicting gods and other mythological figures. Coloured lanterns from Jaipur pour blues and reds and greens onto teak tables. Though Veeraswamy's historical romance is central to its brand, its innovative, seasonal menu proves that it is not time-less but rather constantly negotiating the traditional and the avant-garde, reinventing as well as celebrating the classics. The festival of *Diwali* was marked with a savory, golden curry made from *gulab jamun*, the Indian syrupy sweet. Classics include lamb *rogan josh*, *paneer*, chicken *makhana*. There's a roast duck *vindaloo* too, a twist on the milder Goan original, instead of the fiery British dish popularised in the 1970s as the superlative spice challenge. And yet Veeraswamy insists its food is "rarely found in the restaurants of India let alone the rest of the world." It is, its website professes, "the original Indian gourmet experience." The more inventive parts of the menu almost trump its lavish interior. They remind us that the romance that has come to be expected of Indian restaurants is just a veneer; that it really is the food that has the substance.

London's best Indian restaurants insist upon the authentic and rethink well-known dishes. "I have often thought it such a shame that the Western world has not been let in on the secret of real Indian home cooking," writes London-based Vicky Bhogal in *Cooking Like Mummyji* (2016), co-authored with Atul Kocchar, ex-head chef of Benares, "as though it is a sort of long-standing trick, our last remaining jewel." She explains how Indian home food is much lighter, fresher, healthier, and more fragrant, with a vibrant breadth of flavours.

Grandad's *kali* (black) *daal* is ever-popular at The Punjab, "the first North Indian restaurant in the U.K.," which opened on Neal Street in Covent Garden in 1946. Still, I'm not entirely sure this was what Vicky Bhogal had in mind. The idea of home-cooked food is surely not the same thing as home-cooked food. How would we know when we taste it for the first time? Having once catered to an Indian population during wartime food rationing, The Punjab is a pre-theatre destination today, marked with its smart blue awnings and royal purple inner walls, flanked with old portraits. The food has largely gone unchanged. The *acchari murgh*a, chicken cooked in pickling spices for 48 hours, is the oldest of the restaurant's dishes, a long-standing star of the show. The grandson of the founder can be found in the foyer, suited and sporting a full, white beard.

While history continues to be imitated by new restaurants, in places like The Punjab, it's part of the very fabric of the place. The same year as The Punjab opened, the U.K.'s first Indian high commissioner, Krishna Menon, along with Lady Edwina Mountbatten, wife of the last viceroy of India, and Jawaharlal Nehru, India's first prime minister, founded the India Club for Indians who had moved to London to meet, discuss politics, and have a place they could feel at home. The restaurant is hidden inside the Strand Continental Hotel up a flight of stairs that acts as a time portal. Under the watchful eye of Mahatma, you can tuck into a *paratha* and vegetable curry in the no-frills lunchroom for less than half the price of a bottle of mineral water at some establishments in Mayfair. When the India Club was threatened with being turned into a boutique hotel last year, it received over 20,000 signatures to protect it. The National Trust recently ran an exhibition on the rich social history of what it calls "one of the city's most fascinating community spaces."

The 1960s and 1970s brought much immigration to London, resulting in a wave of Indian restaurant openings in the capital. Many were founded by natives of Bangladesh (previously East Bengal) fleeing the war of independence from Pakistan in '71. Bangladeshis served "Indian cuisine," which, for the British public, conjured up romantic images of the Raj. Serving "Indian cuisine" was better for business. The first *tandoor* was acquired in the Gaylord, established in 1966. Afterwards, others followed, infusing food with the smoky flavour of the charcoal oven. It was this that led to the invention of the chicken *tikka masala*, a British national dish. The Gaylord became an institution, offering time-honoured dishes with little fuss. It recently closed for refurbishment and is due to reopen in late 2019. In 1975, Bishen Dass Anand, who had once cooked for maharajas in Kenya, founded The Brilliant in Southall, a suburban district of West London that affectionately became known as *Chota Punjab* ("Little Punjab"). The Brilliant still lives up to its name. Today, it boasts a cookery school and sells its own pickles and chutneys. Try *methi* chicken with fresh fenugreek leaves, followed by *rasmalai*, the sweet Bengali flavored milk and cheese dessert.

In the 1980s, more restaurants that catered to first- and second-generation British Indians opened outside of the city centre, becoming iconic chains in their own right, such as Saravana Bhavan, which provides low-cost, authentic South Indian food. It has something of a cult following. In the 1990s, South Indian cuisine was further popularised, though it remains less-available than food from the north. Rasa opened in 1994. Its branch in N16 with candy-floss pink walls, stone reliefs, and folk art serves delicious, low-cost, and relatively hard-to-find staples like *rasa idli* (steamed *urad dal*, or black lentil, cakes) and *medhu vadai* (silky dumplings). Welcoming Bollywood stars and celebrity chefs, Rasa is becoming more popular still with the rise of vegetarianism among non-Indians. For many, *these* restaurants are London's iconic Indian ones, not the Indian Accents or even the Dishooms.

In 2001, Tamarind became London's first Indian restaurant to gain a Michelin star. Since, other Indian restaurants have been awarded a star, like Trishna, which serves wild boar *biryani*. At Benares, you can enjoy the same pleasure with lobster, or with saddle of rabbit in Andhra spices finished with a *gulab jamun* brûlée.

I asked Manish Mehrotra why he thinks Indian food is so well-suited to reinvention. "It's interesting for chefs," he told me, with India being "a very versatile place with many regions, temperature, culture, and cuisines—each region with its own, unique delicacies." Today, regional Indian food is celebrated at Michelin-starred restaurants, like Quilon, which focuses on southwest coastal cuisine, and non-traditional eateries alike. Pop-ups and small, affordable diners that don't take reservations serve previously-ignored cuisines or those mixed-in under the heading: "Indian." Places like Little Kolkata are trendy additions to the ever-changing landscape of Soho, where queues curve around buildings.

Old-style curry houses are well-loved but feel dated. "Guests understand Indian food well in London," says Mehrotra. Maybe that's what allows it to keep transforming. In a city where the "Indian restaurant" takes on multifarious forms, its definition is constantly changing. The past has always been intrinsic to Indian cuisine in Britain. It's a long love affair that muses over a history, while always anticipating a future. "Nostalgia is important," Mehrotra says, when I ask him about the train carriage seating in Indian Accent, "But we restrain it to our dishes…Each dish you will try has a story and flavours that take you to its origin...The flavour of each dish," he says, "should justify its roots."

–

THE

House Chai, Dishoom.

From Bombay to London With Love

Words by Sabrina Sucato
Photography by Adam Goldberg and Daniela Velasco

There are places in India and Pakistan, magical places where the intoxicating scent of *khari chai* tea mingles with whiffs of freshly baked biscuits and spicy curry. In these spaces, otherwise known as Irani cafes, oversized mirrors and minimalist furniture create a welcoming world, one that invites guests to sit and stay awhile.

Unfortunately, Irani cafes are a dying breed. Once numbering in the hundreds, they're now few and far between, with most of the stragglers concentrated in cities like Hyderabad and Mumbai.

And London.

In 2010, the city welcomed its first Irani cafe in the form of Dishoom, an unusual little eatery in Covent Garden. Helmed by cousins Shami and Kavi Thakrar, along with brothers Amar and Adarsh Radia, the concept was admittedly a little risky. To start, it noticeably diverged from the traditional approach to Indian cuisine that dominated London food culture. Tired of the polarizing cliches—of incorporating street food into contemporary dining—that Indian fare had become, the partners sought to create something new.

And so, as many good stories go, they began in the past. They found inspiration for Dishoom in 1960s Bombay (now Mumbai), when the popularity of Irani cafes was at its peak. Latching onto the relaxed, social atmosphere typified by those spaces, the quartet brought that ambiance to London proper.

"These [Irani] cafes broke down barriers by bringing people together over food and drink. Their faded elegance welcomed all: courting couples, sweaty taxi-wallas, students, artists, and lawyers," explains co-founder Shami Thakrar. "Telling the story of these cafes is our way of preserving this special part of Bombay heritage."

Of course, in a city that boasted everything from Michelin dining and prim tearooms to international street fare and casual coffee shops, ambiance alone wouldn't sell.

And so they sold the story. They wove

Bhel (cold & crunchy puffed rice), Okra Fries & House Chai, Dishoom.

Spicy Lamb Chops, Chicken Berry Britannia Biryani & Bhel, Dishoom.

INDIA
UNINVITED
GUEST
SIMON
GO BACK

a tale of history, culture, food, and, ultimately, people. For, at their core, the historic Irani cafes were nothing without the denizens who frequented them. With this in mind, the founders of Dishoom told the story of the Bombay subculture to an English community that was largely unaware of its existence.

"When we started doing an Indian breakfast, people properly thought we were mad!" Thakrar recalls. "In truth, it was a bit of a gamble—it just hadn't been done before—but it really took off."

Now, nine years later, Shamil and Kavi oversee seven locations of Dishoom, from the original in Covent Garden to cafes in Carnaby, King's Cross, and Shoreditch. Further afield, it boasts outposts in Edinburgh and, most recently, Manchester. With each new opening, Dishoom concocts a tale around the location, one that sets the scene by looping in history with a sense of place to make the eatery feel less like a restaurant and more like a portal into the past. Even in its slogan "from Bombay with love," which could come off as nothing more than a turn of phrase, Dishoom pays homage to the deep-rooted cultural history at its core.

The breakfast menu, for instance, features everything from the stories behind where the dishes originated to instructions on how to eat them. The note for *Kejriwal*, on the morning roster, reads:
Two fried eggs on chilli cheese toast. A favourite of the well-to-do Willingdon Club, the first such Bombay institution to admit natives; the dish is reputedly named for the member who kept asking for it. (Not to be confused with Arvind Kejriwal, leader of India's Aam Aadmi—common man's—political party.)

Unexpected history primers like these make Dishoom all the more endearing to its food-loving crowd, the kind that comes for the hype and stays for the atmosphere and the chai. They're part of what allows the brand to differentiate itself from London's gastronomic sea and define its existence within the culinary community at large.

Of course, establishment and expansion aren't the only things that happened for Dishoom in its near-decade of existence. The restaurant family ("chain" feels too commercial) has collected a bevy of awards throughout the years, from Best Overall Operator by *Restaurant Magazine* (2017-2018) to listings in the Michelin Guide every year since 2012.

But is Dishoom's niche too narrow? Will the legacy of Irani cafes find longevity here in a way that it didn't in Bombay? Will Londoners one day view Dishoom with tired eyes as their gazes latch onto the next big thing?

Not if Dishoom has its way. If the trail remains clear, the restaurant will continue to spread the legacy of its progenitors in a way that honors history without repeating mistakes. It will tell the stories of a fading culture without losing sight of England's culinary terrain as a whole.

The goal is lofty, to be sure. Yet it nevertheless entices with the possibility of transcendence through ages, communities, and cultures.

"Food is a way of breaking down barriers, and this is at the heart of what we do," Thakrar summarizes. From Bombay with love, indeed.

–

Please Note:-
No Soliciting
No dacoity
No Rowlatt Act
No Salt Tax
No Violence

Turkish Hospitality

Words by Ferhat Dirik

To understand the Turkish food industry and its contribution to London is to accept violence: the slaughter of many lambs converted into kebabs. The sharp slicing of *doner*—a type of kebab cooked on a vertical rotisserie—with a knife the height of a toddler. The frantic chopping of onions. Drunk customers past midnight, unsure of which may fill their appetite more: a meat sandwich dripping in a spicy sauce or a fight with the man behind the counter. All of these jagged edges, small acts of violence, have helped build Turkish restaurant culture within this city, like any historical war and its definition of a new age thereafter. But the real violence we rarely speak of is the tough lives of the men and women who escaped from Turkey in the 1980s in order to shape a better future for their families.

Many arrived in their 20s, escaping their family villages, and their childhood hardships and traumas. The lucky few who went to school would receive beatings from teachers over the smallest discrepancy, and that's before we take into account the dangers within their society. From civil wars concerning Turkish and Kurdish disputes, to street fighting between left-wing and right-wing martyrs, to religious mob beatings between Sunni and Shia. This was the fate which met my parents, a story all too common amongst the elder Turkish and Kurdish communities in London. Life for them when they first moved to London in the 1980s was tough, and with no grasp of English or higher education, it is no small feat that they have helped set up dozens of food establishments in the capital today.

The owners of these establishments brought flavours from all over the Middle East and southern Europe. Because what is a person from Turkey? Like the United States, Turkey is a melting pot. A person from the land of Turkey is Turkish, but they can also be Kurdish (like a majority of "Turkish" restaurant owners in London), Greek, Cypriot, from the Caucasus, Albanian, Persian, Syrian, Iraqi, Georgian, and so on. To list them all would be a U.N. convention. We are all of these things thanks to an active Ottoman Empire that, through victory and defeat, as conquered and conqueror, became a mix of cultures.

Our cuisine is therefore rich. London's restaurants today serve Albanian liver, Lebanese falafel, Cypriot halloumi, Japanese horseradish in the salad, and Jamaican Scotch bonnet peppers in their chili sauce. Yet the taste is unmistakably Turkish. The smokiness of the meats, the crunch of fresh salads, and the rich tomato paste base of the dishes are constants in our cuisine. Quality varies, naturally, but sincere hospitality—that warm welcome and genuine friendliness—is consistent.

These are the fundamental reasons why Londoners took to Turkish cuisine. And perhaps, it was in its name too, Lon*Doner*, a marriage of the hustle and bustle of the city, and the doner kebab. Few things feel as natural to a Londoner as having a feast with your friends, family, and lovers at a Turkish joint—be it a fancy spot with tablecloths, or an unwiped bench inside a takeaway spot around 3 a.m. when your mind wants to keep the night going but your body says, "Ugh, no."

Still, the appreciation between Londoners and the Turkish restaurants that feed them has been less mutual of late. A new BYOB restaurant policy that allows customers to consume alcohol they bring themselves is testing the patience of even the most jovial restaurateurs. Customers are beginning to take advantage of the over-the-top generous nature of Turkish restaurants by bringing their wines, beers (the most infuriating are those who bring their own Turkish Efes, the only beer these restaurants serve), and even their own soft drinks. It's understandable that younger customers still want to be able to eat out without imposing their own overdrafts. But the feeling lingers: Would the same customer find it acceptable to bring such quantities of their own drinks to an Italian, French, British, or any other Central European restaurant? So, why is it okay to do so in Turkish, and to a lesser extent, Bengali eateries? The latter are staunchly Muslim, so they refuse to sell alcohol. Completely understandable. Your average Turk, however, could drink to the bottom of any barrel. Alcohol is a huge part of our culture and we proudly serve good beers and wines. This is perhaps the biggest challenge facing Turkish restaurants and their long-term survival. With rising prices of meat and vegetables in London, alcohol is supposed to be the main profit provider for many restaurants. Take this away and the consequences will be dire. Generosity is within our spirit, as is tolerance, but to what extent?

The second uncertain question involves the next generation of university-educated, second-generation immigrants. Do they keep up the family traditions or venture for a more balanced, less manic life outside the restaurant industry? Who keeps the ball moving when the parent retires, exhausted from a working life beginning at age 12, keen to enjoy the fruits of their labour in their remaining years?

These are the slight potholes on the road for Turkish eateries. The journey is rarely smooth, but at least people from Turkey can now decide which way it goes in London, their new home.

So let the *ocakbasi* (charcoal barbecue) smoke chime out of these restaurant roofs, a thick cloud of fragrant meats no perfume could match. Light up the neon lights of the kebab houses, bringing illumination to the streets until it's dawn. Eat lamb's foot soup at Hala in Green Lanes. Try the seafood and meze over *raki* at Sariyer Balik in Newington Green. Try the kebabs at Mangal 2 before you die. Londanatolia is just beginning.

–

At Your Service

Words by Imogen Lepere
Photography by Adam Goldberg

Being greeted by name as you push open the door. A murmured recommendation that turns out to be exactly to your taste. The gentle flow of conversation in a full dining room. A clean napkin arriving on your lap before you notice that you've dropped the last one. A great restaurant is about much more than just food, and the maître d'hôtel (French for "master of the house," it's often shortened to maître d') is the charismatic presence who makes this seamless experience a reality.

The importance of a maître d' cannot be underestimated. They are the puppet masters who pull the strings of the front of house team without appearing to break a sweat. They not only oversee administrative tasks, like managing reservations and the seating arrangements, but also ensure a great dining atmosphere. They are the friendly faces you see when you arrive—the ones who manage VIPs and regulars, the ones who make first-timers feel welcome—and the calm, smiling presence that helps you into your coat at the end of the evening. Today, the role of the maitre d' is more or less inhabited by the general manager.

Great, classic restaurant-style maître d's, like these faces behind some of London's most iconic restaurants, ensure the whole experience warms your heart.

MATTHEW SILCOCK,
THE WOLSELEY
Housed in a beautiful, Art Deco-style building on Piccadilly, just a few minutes stroll from Buckingham Palace, The Wolseley is a favourite with major players in the media industry and celebrities, such as David Beckham and Kate Moss. Silcock has worked there since 2004. He began his career as a waiter at a small hotel in Liverpool, but his big break was at The Ivy in 2000, where he met Chris Corbin and Jeremy King, the duo behind several top London restaurants. He also worked with Gordon Ramsay for a year at Claridge's, one of London's landmark hotels.

What is a maître d's role? It is to maintain control of the restaurant as well as create the ambience. No one wants to eat in an empty restaurant or a hectic one, so it's up to the maître d' to maintain the perfect balance. As you get to know certain customers, you also remember their likes and dislikes, where they work (and therefore with whom they may prefer to be seated), and more. Then you can discreetly share that information with the team in order to better enhance their experience next time.

How important is it that a maître d's personality matches that of the restaurant? It's more about matching your personality to the customers. You adapt your personality depending on who comes through the door to ensure that particular person feels as comfortable as possible. If you are gregarious and outgoing, yet know when to rein it in, you'll match any restaurant.

How do you handle tricky situations? If there is a problem, it's important to reassure customers that you are doing everything possible to help whilst also thinking quickly on your feet. For example, when I was working at The Ivy, we had two very high-profile regulars who always liked to sit at Table 11. One day, the inevitable happened and both were dining at the same time. Keeping one happy meant offending the other. In the end, we put a bucket on the table and gave our apologies, explaining that there was a leak and the table was out of action for the day.

Is the rise of informal restaurants removing the need for maître d's? In my opinion, having someone on site whose sole purpose is to know the customers personally and be the conductor of the restaurant is priceless.

Can you give any tips for how to bag the best table at your restaurant? If someone makes me laugh, I'll always try to find them a table. Get to know the maître d'—you never know when you might need their help.

EMMANUEL LANDRE,
LE GAVROCHE
Legendary French chef Michel Roux opened this two-Michelin starred restaurant in 1967, passing over the reins to his son Michel Roux, Jr. in 1991. Amazingly, it is still considered the premier address

Right: Matthew Silcock, The Wolseley.

for formal French dining in London and has produced culinary legends such as Marco Pierre White and Gordon Ramsay. Emmanuel Landre achieved his BAC Technique Hotelier at Lycée Hotelier de Thonon Les Bains in 1997. He went straight to Le Gavroche as commis waiter in 1998, progressing to maître d' and assistant manager over the next ten years before landing the general manager position at the restaurant in 2008.

What is a maître d's role? The best recipe for a restaurant is great food, polished service, and an effervescent atmosphere—and you need a full restaurant to deliver this. I oversee all of the reservations, making sure my team and I work hard to keep Le Gavroche full.

Is a great meal about more than just food? The difference between a good restaurant and a great restaurant is the detail. Bad food can be recovered by excellent service but good food can be damaged by bad service. We aren't "the show," but we make it the perfect show for our clients.

Define the perfect customer. The perfect customer is not the one spending the most; it's the person coming in with a smile and a desire to have a good time. Sometimes we need to break the ice when clients come in for the first time, and it's the duty of the maître d' to engage in conversation. But we also provide almost invisible service once someone feels at home.

Is the rise of informal restaurants removing the need for maître d'? There is always a need for good management and underestimating the importance of service is a mistake. The maître d' puts the "welcome" into the restaurant business—and that role should be as important in casual dining as it is in fine dining.

Can you give any tips for how to bag the best table at your restaurant? The only way is to become a regular, whether it's once a week, once a month, or once a year. We welcome back our regulars with personalised service, whether it's an awareness of allergies, their birthdays, or their favourite table.

GORDANA SHERIFF,
SCOTT'S

Among the five oldest restaurants in London, Scott's has been the last word in market-fresh seafood since 1851. It still attracts one of the most glamorous crowds in Mayfair (recent visitors include Tom Hanks and Charles Saatchi) and its terrace tables on Mount Street are among the most sought after in London. Gordana's first job was as a 17-year-old hat check girl at Joe Allen, a West End legend, where she spent hours watching the maître d'. She went on to become assistant general manager of the legendary members club, The Groucho, which she describes as "huge fun and full of colourful characters." After stints at 192 Restaurant, J Sheekey, and The Ivy, she became senior maître d' at Scott's in 2014.

What is a maître d's role? The most important aspect of the job is to be welcoming and able to read each customer's needs. Sometimes, in the case of business lunches and dinners, guests may require a more formal service and not much interaction; other times, they may want to laugh and chat.

What attracted you to being front-of-house rather than a chef? Hospitality is in my blood. My father was a chef and our house was always full of guests that, as a teenager, I had to look after. I found that I enjoyed the social interaction and bustle of the job.

How do you handle very well-known customers? The well-known generally come to the restaurant to relax, so we always make sure that we have the table ready and whisk them in quickly to avoid attracting unwanted attention. While I was working at the Groucho Club, I had to smuggle a very well-known American singer-songwriter to her car via the rickety fire escape due to the huge amount of paparazzi outside the main entrance.

Who are your maître d' heroes? The legendary Elena Salvoni of Elena's L'Etoile in Charlotte Street and my boss at the Groucho Club, Liam Carson. Sadly, neither is still with us, but both had the extraordinary ability to make everyone feel special.

Can you give any tips for how to bag the best table at your restaurant? The best thing to do is to mention preferred seating at the time of booking and to perhaps book for the quieter times when it is more likely that the request can be met.

MANNY TSINAS,
THE IVY

This star-studded spot in Covent Garden has been a theatreland favourite for more than a century and has counted Laurence Olivier, Tom Cruise, and Princess Diana amongst its regulars over the years. The Ivy's signature shepherd's pie is also widely regarded as the best in London. Manny joined as maître d' in 2011 after many years as Head of European Customer Services for Gucci. He cut his teeth in the hospitality world in his home city of Montreal, Canada where he oversaw the opening of two well-received restaurants before bringing his skills to London.

What is a maître d's role? The maître d' has two fundamental roles. The first is to be the warm-up act, to set the tone when customers first arrive, and the second is to act as a go-between, a channel of communication between the customers and the kitchen. As such, a maître d' can have a massive impact on the atmosphere of the restaurant, as well as a guest's overall experience.

How do you handle very well-known customers? When a Hollywood star comes in with their spouse, it serves you well to get the greeting right. A star always appreciates it when you don't ignore the person they are with.

Is a great meal about more than just food? If so, what? There are lots of factors that all hang in careful harmony. Lighting, table size, acoustics, comfort, and the ability to have a conversation without being interrupted are all crucial elements.

What attracted you to being front of house rather than a chef? I would rather stand at the desk speaking to customers than be in front of a hot stove cooking on a tight deadline. The pressures are very different, and I know which I prefer.

Can you give any tips for readers on how to bag the best table at your restaurant? Come often, be nice, and don't be too demanding. The best customers are the ones who know what they want but go about getting it with good manners.

JOEL GROVES,
J SHEEKEY
J Sheekey's pillar box-red facade has brightened up St. Martin's Court, a historic alleyway near Leicester Square, since 1893. Its Victorian interiors make a charming setting in which to enjoy oysters and Champagne as photographs of the many famous former patrons look on. Joel joined the Caprice restaurant group in 2011 and has been maitre d' of J Sheekey since 2013. Before that, he spent three years as beverage manager at ultra-luxe department store Harvey Nichols.

How important is it that a maître d's personality matches that of the restaurant? I think one influences the other. We have two very different environments at J Sheekey, the Restaurant and The Atlantic Bar. I tend to be much more gregarious in The Atlantic Bar as it's more relaxed and customers are mostly sat on stools, so you're at eye level throughout their experience. The Restaurant is more formal, so I connect with guests on arrival, leave them to it, and then reconnect before they leave.

Is a great meal about more than just food? It's about the whole experience, including having a genuine connection with the person serving you. I love the feeling I get when I make a difference to someone's experience, even if it's just suggesting a particular dish or delivering something special to mark an occasion.

What attracted you to being front of house rather than a chef? I think front- or back-of-house chooses you. I actually trained as a chef but hated it. I was 19, working nights, and found it really difficult to socialise, so I got a temporary job in the Cafe at Harvey Nichols instead. I loved the customer-facing aspect. At J Sheekey, you meet a very eclectic clientele and the stories they have of the restaurant are fascinating. It has played a key role in many Londoners' lives for generations.

Who are your maître d' heroes? John Andrews, my predecessor at J Sheekey, and Sian Cox, of OXO Brasserie, have been my two biggest influences. They are both very theatrical and tenacious, no matter what a situation throws at them.

Can you give any tips for readers on how to bag the best table at your restaurant? Everyone's image of the perfect table is different. Some like booths, corners, windows, or bar stools, so if you don't like the one you have, just ask. It won't always be possible, but I would always try and offer an alternative if asked politely.

–

CAFFÈ

Rhubarb & Cardamon Creme Brûlée, Rosemary & Sea Salt Bread Sticks, Baguette, Pophams Bakery.

A Sweet Weekend

Words by John Moore
Photography by Daniela Velasco

Would a London weekend without a pastry or bread still taste as sweet? For London resident John Moore, days off work without exquisite, freshly baked goods miss the point: London is a brilliant city for hip bakeries. Nestled amid charming markets and in quirky old buildings in London's backstreets, the city's new guard of bakers slow the pace down—welcoming visitors to spaces where breathing hot dough-scented air and biting into laminated pastries provide momentary respite from a smartphone-dominated world. Here, Moore details the rise of his favorite spots, the bakeries that make his Saturdays and Sundays feel like weekly holidays.

LILY VANILLI

"What a beautiful spectacle!" I overheard the man behind me say while I was in line at Lily Vanilli. The lady with him looked confused and responded with a tone of disbelief, "You like the market today?" "No, the market's for you," he replied, as though he were stating the obvious. "How about you go back out there and enjoy it while I stay in here and enjoy these sweets." I laughed; I was proud of his recommendation.

Nestled away in the corner of a late-1800s wood workshop, just behind the Columbia Road Flower Market, is the bustling and energetic home of Lily Vanilli Bakery. Inside, where woodturning tools once stood, mixers and ovens now whiz and hum as Lily Jones (better known as Vanilli) and her team whip up colorful sweet and savoury baked goods.

I live above the bakery where I hear the carts rolling across the cobblestones each day, carrying fresh ingredients destined to be transformed. Except for Sunday, the space is Jone' studio, where you will find her creating her bespoke cakes. On Sunday, she converts it into her weekly pop-up shop. To keep it fresh, Jones constantly changes the line-up.

My ideal Sunday morning starts with any pastry that includes her chocolate ganache, or one of her must-try brownies—they are addictive—along with a hot cup of coffee. Curious to watch the market's early happenings, I sit at the table just outside in The Courtyard and watch as the market comes to life. I wish every day could start like this.

Everything does taste delicious. And all of the pastries are exceptionally beautiful. The weekly seasonal menu does, in fact, outdo itself week after week. But, most of all, I love how the bakery makes me feel. From the moment I see the "Vanilli" light bulb sign sparkling behind the counter, I feel energized and alive. That is what keeps me going back.

I also have deep respect for how Jones gives back so generously to the community. She created the #BakeForSyria campaign to help UNICEF fundraise to protect the children of Syria. The beautiful charity cookbook she curated, #BakeForSYRIA, is filled with Syrian-inspired recipes from an amazing collection of bakers. The Little Double Chocolate Tahini Cakes and the Tahini and Cardamom Buns, which came from that effort, are currently my two favorite recipes.

Jones also founded the annual YBFs (Young British Foodies) awards and ceremony, which celebrates new butchers, bakers, and cocktail-makers for their talents. The support and encouragement generated from events like these, sprinkled with a dash of competition, builds camaraderie and a community obsessed with making good food great.

POPHAMS BAKERY

Inside what was once an old pharmacy, Pophams Bakery serves the finest, flakiest croissants I have ever tasted. Ollie Gold and head chef Florin Grama, the 2018 YBF award-winning baker, have built a bakery that seems to get all of the details *right*: the location is superb; the simple interior is comfortable and inviting; and the beautiful ceramics escalate the experience of a pastry on a plate to a higher level. And then there are the seemingly infinite number of layers in the pastries and croissants. The more crispy, laminated layers, the better, especially those in the "Bacon & Maple," a blend of soft pastry, savory meat, and a hint of sweetness from the maple syrup. These go quickly—one has to get there early to snag one. For something just as delicious without meat, one can never go wrong with the rosemary and sea salt twist. While an idyllic day can begin by eating one at Pophams' outdoor tables in the sun, I especially like to bring the pastries home to supplement with a slice of cheese and a glass of wine.

At Pophams, I live for the weekend specials. While the bakery is open daily, the extra items sold on Saturday and Sunday are worth the wait. I still think about the recent Triple Chocolate: chocolate hazelnut fudge, chocolate custard, and chocolate crumb, held tightly together with a flaky pastry crust. The Hazelnut Praline weekend special is what weekends were made for: a sandwich filled with dollops of hazelnut cream that suspend thin layers of croissant pastry that are garnished with sliced toasted almonds. It's hard to remember the stresses of the week once you bite in.

VIOLET

Several blocks north of Hackney's London Fields Park is one of London's quaintest streets called Wilton Way. A block west of the little cluster of shops, you will stumble across a humble white, box-shaped building, which houses Claire Ptak's ever-popular Violet Cakes.

Its simplicity makes it feel as if it's a hidden spot on a back street of Tokyo rather than London. On the side of the building, several garden tables and chairs huddle along an old brick wall with perfect patina. The green graphic letters spelling "Violet" on the side of the building set an organic, grassroots tone. It makes me want to pull up a seat and linger.

Inside of this very tiny space is a bakery-market, where Ptak has balanced the baking activities on the left with the shopping activities on the right. In the middle, the two intermingle in what looks like a tentative waltz, as customers side-step one another to let the bakers pass and vice versa.

Yet no matter how busy it gets, the bakery hums calmly through it. The noisiest place is inside my head as I debate what to try. The choices are abundant, displayed simply in a vintage wood-and-glass men's shirt display case. I feel nostalgic each time I see it, as it looks nearly identical to the one in the store where I bought my first suit. I giggle to myself, as it looks much happier with colorful cakes than the one I remember holding neatly folded white shirts.

Of everything magical at Violet, I am most in love with the seasonal buttercream icing—I could have it on anything. It is so soft and fresh with the flavor of the ingredients so pronounced. It is Ptak's ability to highlight flavors that I value most. I prefer cakes that are less sweet, and Ptak has mastered that, swapping excess sugar for high-quality chocolate and organic fruits and nuts that taste more like the raw ingredients than an oversweet extraction. I recently took a friend there who was visiting London and he said several times, "This chocolate tastes amazing. I have never tasted anything like this before."

The flavors all come together perfectly in her chocolate caramel rum cake, with each ingredient distinct yet harmoniously blended into a rich, moist cake. Alternate bites with sips of coffee, and tell me that isn't a perfect start to the day.

I had my first Violet experience when Ptak had a stall at Broadway Market on Saturday. I started the weekend with a cinnamon bun made with her quick bread recipe. I loved both the noticeable spice of her cinnamon flavor and their organic shape. Since then, Ptak moved to her current space in Hackney where she is open daily, except for a brief closure last year, when she was asked by Prince Harry and Meghan Markle to create their lemon and elderflower flavored wedding cake—which was topped with my favorite buttercream icing.

–

1
4
9

Prune, Oat and Spelt Scone, Violet.

Hazelnut Praline, Rhubarb & Cardamon Creme Brûlée, Rosemary & Sea Salt Bread Sticks, Baguette, Pophams Bakery.

appendix

00
12:51
107 Upper St,
London N1 1QN, UK

40 Maltby Street
40 Maltby St,
London SE1 3PA, UK

67 Pall Mall
67 Pall Mall, St. James's,
London SW1Y 5ES, UK

A
Amaya
Halkin Arcade, Lowndes St, Belgravia,
London SW1X 8JT, UK

Atariya Foods Golders Green
15-16 Monkville Ave,
London NW11 0AL, UK

Attica
74 Glen Eira Rd, Ripponlea
VIC 3185, Australia

B
Berry Bros. & Rudd
Hamilton Close, Houndmills
Basingstoke, RG21 6YB, UK

Benares
12a, Berkeley Square, Mayfair,
London W1J 6BS, UK

Black Axe Mangal
156 Canonbury Rd,
London N1 2UP, UK

Bombay Bustle
29 Maddox St, Mayfair,
London W1S 2PA, UK

Brat
4 Redchurch St,
London E1 6JL, UK

Brawn
49 Columbia Rd,
London E2 7RG, UK

Bright
1 Westgate St,
London E8 3RL, UK

C
Chutney Mary
73 St James's St, St. James's,
London SW1A 1PH, UK

Cinnamon Bazaar
28 Maiden Ln, Covent Garden,
London WC2E 7JS, UK

Climpson's Arch
374 Helmsley Pl, Hackney,
London E8 3SB, UK

Cornerstone
3 Prince Edward Rd,
London E9 5LX, UK

D
Death by Pizza
Netil Market, 13-23 Westgate St,
London E8 3RL, UK

Dishoom
12 Upper St Martin's Ln,
London WC2H 9FB, UK

Dishoom
22 Kingly St, Soho,
London W1B 5QB, UK

Dishoom
4 Derry St, Kensington,
London W8 5SE, UK

Dishoom
5 Stable St, Kings Cross,
London N1C 4AB, UK

Dishoom
7 Boundary St,
London E2 7JE, UK

Dozo
32, Old Compton St,
London W1D 4TP, UK

G
George Inn
The George Inn Yard, 77 Borough High St,
London SE1 1NH, UK

Gymkhana
42 Albemarle St, Mayfair,
London W1S 4JH, UK

H
Hala
29-30 Grand Parade, Harringay,
London N4 1LG, UK

Harvey Nichols
109-125 Knightsbridge, Belgravia,
London SW1X 7RJ, UK

Harwood Arms
Walham Grove, Fulham,
London SW6 1QP, UK

Hix Soho
66-70 Brewer Street,
London W1F 9UP, UK

Holborn Dining Room
252 High Holborn,
London WC1V 7EN, UK

Ho Lee Fook
蘇豪 1-5號地下, Elgin St,
Central, Hong Kong

Hugh Lowe Farms
215 Willow Wents, Mereworth,
Maidstone ME18 5NF, UK

I
Ikoyi
1 St James's Market, St. James's,
London SW1Y 4AH, UK

Indian Accent
16 Albemarle St, Mayfair,
London W1S 4HW, UK

J
Jikoni
19 - 21 Blandford St, Marylebone,
London W1U 3DG, UK

J Sheekey
33-35 St Martin's Ct, Covent Garden,
London WC2N 4AL, UK

K
Kitty Fisher's
10 Shepherd Market, Mayfair,
London W1J 7QF, UK

Kyseri
64 Grafton Way, Bloomsbury,
London W1T 5DN, UK

L
L' Etoile
73 Westbourne Grove,
London W2 4UJ, UK

Le Gavroche
43 Upper Brook St, Mayfair,
London W1K 7QR, UK

Leroy
18 Phipp St,
London EC2A 4NU, UK

Lily Vanilli Bakery
6 The Courtyard, Ezra Street
Tower Hamlets, London N1 8PF, UK

Little Kolkata
51-53 Shelton St, Covent Garden,
London WC2H 9JU, UK

Lokhandwala
93 Charlotte St, Bloomsbury,
London W1T 4PY, UK

London's Basement Sate
8 Broadwick St, Soho,
London W1F 8HN, UK

Lyle's
Tea Building, 56 Shoreditch High St,
London E1 6JJ, UK

M
Maitre Choux
15 Harrington Rd,
Kensington, London SW7 3ES, UK

Maitre Choux
60 Dean St, Soho,
London W1D 6AW, UK

Mangal 2
4 Stoke Newington Rd, Hackney Downs,
London N16 8BH, UK

Marksman Public House
254 Hackney Rd,
London E2 7SJ, UK

Mission Chinese
171 E Broadway,
New York, NY 10002, US

Mugaritz
Aldura Gunea Aldea, 20, 20100
Errenteria, Gipuzkoa, Spain

N

Nathan Outlaw
22-24 Basil St, Knightsbridge,
London SW3 1AT, UK

Noble Fine Liquour
27 Broadway Market,
London E8 4PH, UK

Noble Rot Wine Bar & Restaurant
51 Lamb's Conduit St,
London WC1N 3NB, UK

O

Oklava
74 Luke St,
London EC2A 4PY, UK

OXO Brasserie
Oxo Tower Wharf, Barge House St, South Bank,
London SE1 9PH, UK

P

P. Franco
107 Lower Clapton Rd, Lower Clapton,
London E5 0NP, UK

Pie Room at Holborn Dining Room
252 High Holborn,
London WC1V 7EN, UK

Pophams Bakery
19 Prebend St,
London N1 8PF, UK

Q

Quilon
41 Buckingham Gate, Westminster,
London SW1E 6AF, UK

R

Raki
56 Green Lanes, Stoke Newington,
London N16 9NH, UK

Rasa
55 Stoke Newington Church St, Stoke Newington,
London N16 0AR, UK

Rochelle Canteen
16 Playground Gardens,
London E2 7FA, UK

S

Sager + Wilde
193 Hackney Rd,
London E2 8JL, UK

Saravana Bhavan
300 High St N, East Ham,
London E12 6SA, UK

Sariyer Balik
56 Green Lanes, Stoke Newington,
London N16 9NH, UK

Scott's
20 Mount St, Mayfair,
London W1K 2HE, UK

Septime
80 Rue de Charonne, 75011
Paris, France

St. John
26 St John St, Clerkenwell,
London EC1M 4AY, UK

St. John Bread and Wine
94-96 Commercial St,
London E1 6LZ, UK

T

The Admiral Codrington
17 Mossop St, Chelsea,
London SW3 2LY, UK

The Brilliant
72-76 Western Rd,
Southall UB2 5DZ, UK

The Cake Store
111 Sydenham Rd,
London SE26 5UA, UK

The Clove Club
Shoreditch Town Hall, 380 Old St,
London EC1V 9LT, UK

The Conduit
40 Conduit St, Mayfair,
London W1S 2YQ, UK

The Delaunay
55 Aldwych, Holborn,
London WC2B 4BB, UK

The Draper's Arms
44 Barnsbury St,
London N1 1ER, UK

The Fat Duck
94-96 Commercial St,
London E1 6LZ, UK

The Gaylord
141 Manchester Rd, Isle of Dogs,
London E14 3DN, UK

The Groucho Club
45 Dean St, Soho,
London W1D 4QB, UK

The Harrow
Whitefriars St,
London EC4Y 8JJ, UK

The Ivy
1-5 West St,
London WC2H 9NQ, UK

The Lamb and Flag
24 James St, Marylebone,
London W1U 1EL, UK

The Lily Vanilli Bakery
6, The Courtyard, Ezra St,
London E2 7RH, UK

The Prospect of Whitby
57 Wapping Wall, St Katharine's & Wapping,
London E1W 3SH, UK

The Punjab
80 Neal St,
London WC2H 9PA, UK

The River Café
Thames Wharf, Rainville Rd, Hammersmith,
London W6 9HA, UK

The Spaniards Inn
Spaniards Rd, Hampstead,
London NW3 7JJ, UK

The Wolseley
160 Piccadilly, St. James's,
London W1J 9EB, UK

U

Uyen Luu
Unit 32 (3rd floor); Regent Studios, 8 Andrews Road, Hackney, London E8 4QN, UK

V

Veeraswamy
Victory House, 99-101 Regent St, Mayfair,
London W1B 4RS, UK

Violet Bakery
47 Wilton Way,
London E8 3ED, UK

W

Wildair
142 Orchard St,
New York, NY 10002, US

Y

Ye Olde Cheshire Cheese
145 Fleet St,
London EC4A 2BU, UK

Young Vegans Pie Shop
60 Camden Lock Pl, Camden Town,
London NW1 8AF, UK

A°

www.ambrosiamag.com
•
instagram/ambrosiamagazine
twitter/ambrosiamag
facebook/ambrosiamag